Onigiri

fun & creative recipes for Japanese rice balls

Sanae Inada

Marshall Cavendish
Cuisine

All photos by Joshua Tan, Elements By The Box

Copyright © 2012 Marshall Cavendish International (Asia) Private Limited
First published 2012 as Simply Onigiri
This new edition published 2018

Published by Marshall Cavendish Cuisine
An imprint of Marshall Cavendish International

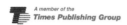
A member of the
Times Publishing Group

Other Marshall Cavendish Offices:
Marshall Cavendish Corporation, 99 White Plains Road, Tarrytown NY 10591-9001, USA • Marshall
Cavendish International (Thailand) Co Ltd. 253 Asoke, 12th Flr, Sukhumvit 21 Road, Klongtoey Nua,
Wattana, Bangkok 10110, Thailand • Marshall Cavendish (Malaysia) Sdn Bhd, Times Subang, Lot 46,
Subang Hi-Tech Industrial Park, Batu Tiga, 40000 Shah Alam, Selangor Darul Ehsan, Malaysia

Marshall Cavendish is a trademark of Times Publishing Limited

National Library Board, Singapore Cataloguing-in-Publication Data

Name(s): Inada, Sanae.
Title: Onigiri : fun and creative recipes for Japanese rice balls / Sanae Inada.
Description: Second edition. | Singapore : Marshall Cavendish Cuisine, [2018] | Previously published as:
Simply onigiri: fun and creative recipes for Japanese rice balls. 2012.
Identifier(s): OCN 1042277000 | ISBN 978-981-48-2849-9 (paperback)
Subject(s): LCSH: Cooking, Japanese. | Cooking (Rice). | LCGFT: Cookbooks.
Classification: DDC 641.5952--dc23

Printed in Malaysia

To those who love Japanese food

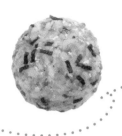

Contents

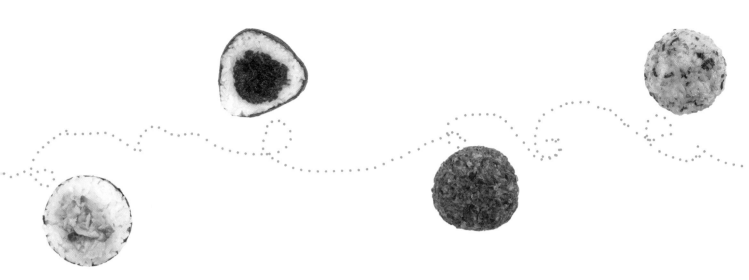

Acknowledgements

I want to thank my parents, Kaoru and Mitsuo Inada.
Our meals have always been full of laughter and silly jokes.
My parents taught me the importance of effort, creativity,
kindness, positiveness and being yourself.

The team at Marshall Cavendish International (Asia) —
I had great fun working with you.

Joshua Tan, thank you for shooting beautiful pictures.

I also want to thank everyone who has encouraged me, told me
anything positive, and shared great conversation and laughter
over our meals. Your words, smiles, tears and kindness inspire
me in my cooking and baking as well as in my life.

Celebrity chef Anthony Bourdain once said, "Food is everything
we are. It's an extension of nationalist feeling, ethnic feeling,
your personal history, your province, your region, your tribe,
your grandma. It's inseparable from those from the get-go."

In this sense, I would like to thank my awesome grandparents.
They are not here any more but I have fantastic memories of
time spent with them. My grandma began teaching me how to
make traditional dishes when I was little. My grandpa gave me
my first sip of beer when I was five. They were the centre of
their community and the source of my quirky sense of humour.

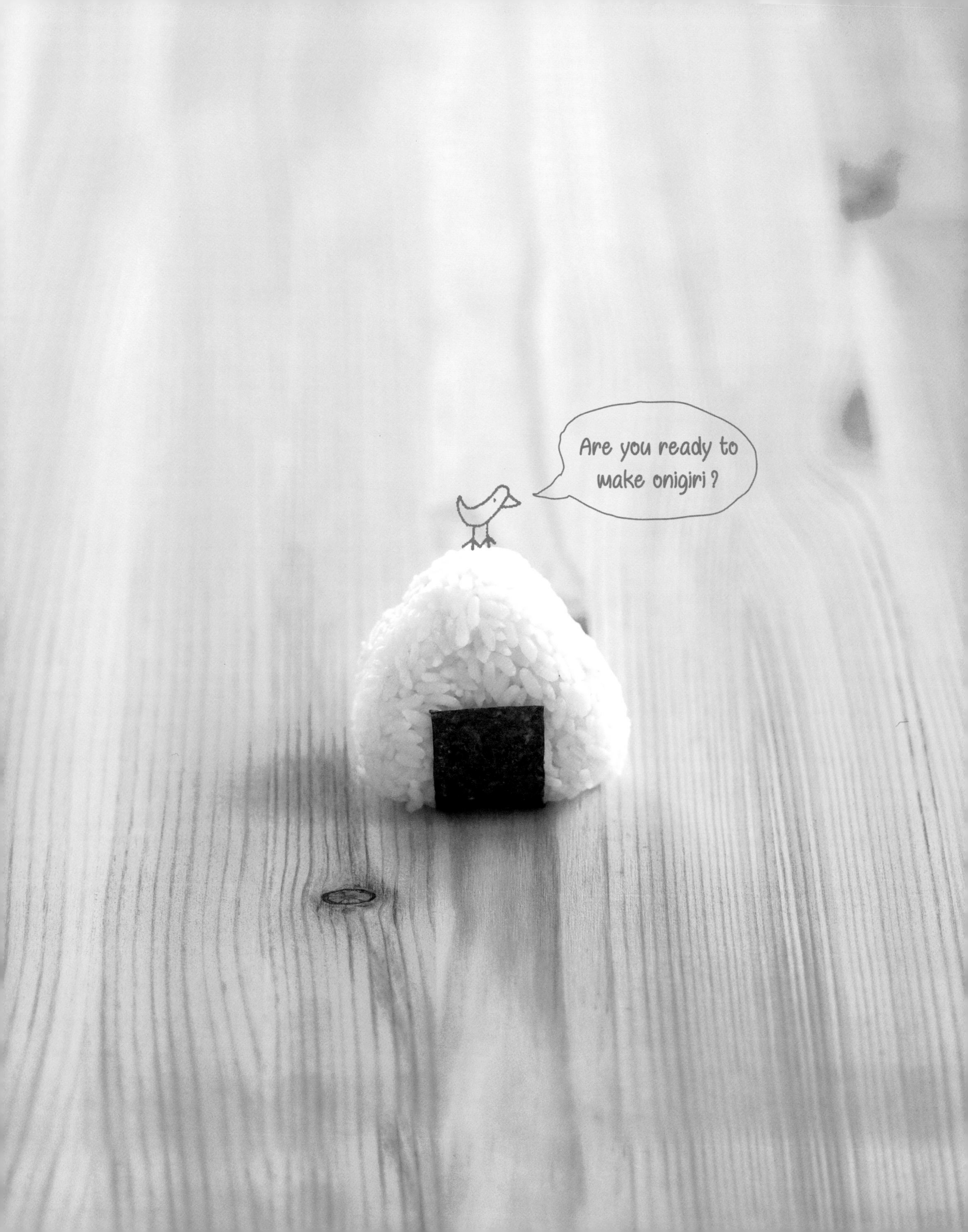
Are you ready to make onigiri ?

Introduction

Do you have a favourite food that is so simple to make but hard to find at restaurants?

Onigiri is one of those dishes. Onigiri is Japanese soul food. You can discover Japanese culture and seasons through the rice ball. Ingredients that go into it are often seasonal and some regions specialise in certain kinds of onigiri. For example, *tenmusu*, onigiri filled with tempura prawns, is a speciality of Nagoya city, while luncheon meat onigiri was very popular in Okinawa before becoming well-liked all over Japan.

I hope this book inspires you to create your own onigiri and step into a Japanese culinary journey. All the ingredients in the book are easily found at your local or Japanese supermarket. The recipes are very simple (even those made with many ingredients) yet you can enjoy authentic Japanese flavours at home. Feel free to adjust the amount of ingredients used to suit your taste. Every individual has his or her own preferences, so use the recipes in this cookbook as guides and suggestions. However, please keep in mind three basic points to make delicious onigiri:

Use Japanese short grain rice
Use natural sea salt
Put in lots of love

Let's put on our aprons, roll up our sleeves and wash our hands!

Are you ready to make onigiri?

Sanae

What is Onigiri?

Onigiri is a rice ball that comes in a variety of shapes and can be filled with different ingredients

You can eat them for breakfast, as a snack or even pack them into a bento box to bring along for picnics. In this sense, onigiri is the Japanese equivalent of a sandwich or Cornish pasty. Every Japanese has his or her favourite onigiri and each region in Japan has its own special version. My favourites are umeboshi and *tarako* (salted cod roe) onigiri my mother makes.

Onigiri has been part of Japan's culinary offering for centuries. The Japanese believe that the humble rice ball reflects the time and place where the person making the onigiri lives, his/her family and cooking philosophy, and that all these will be passed on to the person eating the onigiri.

Traditionally, onigiri is made with bare hands and the rice has to be very hot when you mould it into shape. Even when your hands become red from the heat, you cannot complain! It sounds funny but this is the key to making delicious onigiri. When you mould the rice, wet your hands and spread a pinch of salt evenly on your palms and fingers. When the hot rice is transferred to your hands, the water evaporates and forms a thin salty layer over the rice ball. This salty layer keeps moisture and air inside while preventing germs from multiplying. This is why you can carry onigiri around even during the hot summer months. This layer of salt also keeps the rice moist—even when it is cold, so you can still enjoy the great taste of the rice and the delicious fillings hours after making the onigiri.

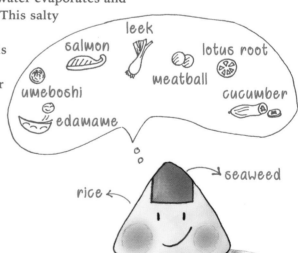

A Short History of Onigiri

The history of onigiri goes back to the Yayoi period dating between 300 BC and 300 AD.

We know this because a carbonised chunk of rice was found at an archaeological site. It was subsequently claimed as the oldest onigiri in Japan. Originally, glutinous rice (*mochi*) was used for onigiri but from the end of Kamakura period, between 1192 and 1333, Japanese short grain rice (*uruchi-mai*) was used. The custom of wrapping onigiri with seaweed started during the Edo period between 1603 and 1867.

Onigiri has a range of regional variations. In Japan, these rice balls are called by various names. Onigiri, from the word *nigiru* (which means 'to grab'), *omusubi* (which means 'to tie' or 'to knot') and *nigirimeshi* (which means 'to grab rice or food') are all names for the rice ball. In general, onigiri and *omusubi* are interchangeable and widely recognised in Japan and around the world. Onigiri also come in a variety of forms such as triangle, round, barrel and square shapes.

There are many old Japanese stories that feature onigiri. One of my favourite stories is called *Omusubi Kororin. Kororin* is an onomatopoeia of the rolling sound.

Once upon a time, there was an old farmer and his wife.
One day, the old farmer was cutting trees in the mountains as usual.
At lunchtime, he sat down on a tree stump to have the lunch that his wife
prepared. When he opened the omusubi *wrapped with bamboo leaf, one*
of the rice balls dropped and started rolling down the hill. The old farmer
tried running after the rice ball but it fell into a very small hole. Just then,
the old man heard a happy voice coming from the small hole. The voice
was singing "Omusubi kororin sutton ton!" He was very surprised and
dropped one more omusubi *into the hole and again he heard, "Omusubi*
kororin sutton ton!" The farmer continued dropping one omusubi *after*
another into the hole so he could continue hearing the happy song. Soon
after, he too fell into the hole.

Inside, the farmer saw a nest of mice having a party. They thanked the old man for giving them the delicious omusubi. In return, the mice offered the old farmer a big box and a small box. The old farmer chose the small one and thanked the mice and headed home. Together with his wife, the old farmer opened the small box and to their delight, found money and treasure inside.

A neighbouring farmer heard this story and went to the mountain with omusubi. He kicked one omusubi into a small hole to see if he could hear the song. When he heard the happy singing, he jumped into the hole and asked for presents. The mice asked him to choose the big box or small box and the greedy farmer grabbed both boxes and tried to leave. However, the mice bit him and the old man returned home with nothing but bites all over his body.

Types of Rice

Generally, there are three types of rice available worldwide—Japonica, Indica and Javanica rice. It is very important that you use Japanese short grain rice when making onigiri.

The short and round Japonica rice is cultivated in Japan, Korea, northern China and North America. The grains become sticky when cooked, helping the onigiri to keep its shape even after you bite into it.

The Indica variety is long and narrow and does not become sticky when cooked. It is grown and harvested in China, Vietnam, Thailand, Myanmar, Bangladesh, India and North America. Javanica rice grains are larger compared to the other two varieties. It is grown and harvested in South East Asia, Italy and Brazil.

There are over 270 varieties of rice in Japan. Widely known types are Koshihikari, Hitomebore, Hinohikari and Akitakomachi. You can also choose white (polished) rice or brown (unpolished) rice. Brown rice is a healthier option as it is the whole grain with the rice bran which contains more minerals, vitamins and fibre. If you visit a Japanese supermarket, you will find a rice polishing machine where you can select the polishing percentage such as 100% for *hakumai* (white rice), 50% for *gobuzuki* and no polishing for *genmai* (brown rice). The by-product of polished rice, rice bran or *nuka*, is used to make *nukazuke* pickles, cosmetics and fertiliser. Using *nuka* for scrubbing your face or body is purported to make your skin smooth and healthy!

Japanese rice has a lower percentage of a type of starch called amylose, which helps to maintain the taste of cooked rice even after it has cooled down. This is the reason why Japanese rice is good for onigiri. On the other hand, *mochi* rice (glutinous rice) has almost no amylose but contains amylopectin, which makes the rice extremely sticky.

How to keep Rice

Rice is a dried food and it is very sensitive to heat and humidity. In general, rice should be stored in an airtight container and kept in a cool place.

If you have polished rice, it is best to use it within 2 weeks. You can keep brown rice for up to a year. The best place to store rice is in the refrigerator. However, if you don't want to take up space in the refrigerator, keep the rice in a cool, dark place and place a red chilli in the container. The chilli will keep bugs away.

I have heard some strategies for keeping cooked leftover rice. In my experience, the best way is to freeze it. The key to this process is to wrap one portion of hot rice in cling wrap and store in the freezer. By wrapping hot rice, it will keep the moisture intact. Make sure you use heatproof cling wrap. When you would like to reheat the rice, simply pop it into the microwave oven and heat. Keeping rice in the refrigerator is fine if you wish to consume the rice within 2 days. Heating the rice with a sprinkle of water or sake will revive the rice nicely. You can also steam the rice to warm it up. Just remember to remove the cling wrap before heating up the rice!

The newer models of rice cookers now come with an ingenious function for keeping rice. Some of them allow you to keep the rice in the device for up to 2 days without drying it out or losing its taste. In the old days, people in Japan used an *ohitsu*. It is a wooden container made from the bark of the cypress tree. Traditionally, rice was transferred into the *ohitsu* from the cooker. The rice is kept covered in this wooden container until it is served. What the container does is to remove unnecessary moisture and keep the rice fresh. Even during summer, it keeps rice fresh for a surprisingly long time. In Japan, the *ohitsu* is always placed next to the mother whose duty is to serve the family.

Itadakimasu and Gochisousama

Itadakimasu is a Japanese greeting said before eating and gochisousama is the greeting said after a meal.

When I think about the meaning of these phrases, it makes me feel warm and fuzzy. The literal meaning of *itadakimasu* is "to be given". The word belongs to a group of honorific terms known as *kenjo-go*. These terms are used to address people who are of a higher ranking than oneself. *Itadakimasu* originated from the action of being given food from a person of a higher rank or getting food from offerings. It also has a meaning of giving thanks to nature and to the people who have given the food to you. In a way, it is about appreciating the life of plants and animals, and also being thankful to the people who prepared and cooked your food.

The meaning of *gochisousama* is tricky because if you translate it literally, it means "it was amazing food". However, the meaning of this greeting is a little more complicated. If you break up the word, *chi* and *sou* in *gochisou*, it means "to run". In the olden days, people were running around risking their lives to get food to serve special guests. This greeting refers to these people who have made huge efforts in preparing meals. Just like *itadakimasu*, *gochisousama* refers to appreciating and thanking the people who have prepared the meal.

I must confess that up till I was 16 years old, I thought these words were only meant for my mother and other people who made my meals. When I went to America for the first time as an exchange student, my host family asked me the meaning of these greetings and I wasn't able to answer the question. When I looked it up after returning to Japan, I found that these words have a much deeper meaning and I wrote a letter to my host family to answer the question. Since then, saying *itadakimasu* and *gochisousama* have become much more special to me.

Itadakimasu

Gochisousama

The Power of Umeboshi

If you enjoy eating Japanese food, you would probably be familiar with umeboshi.

I use to pickle my own umeboshi every year when I was living in Tokyo and it was one of my favourite seasonal preparations of the year. Ume plum is in season around June. Whenever I visited my grandmother in the summer, it was always around the time she dried ume plum on bamboo baskets, placing them at the corridor facing her garden. I loved lying on this corridor for naps. Thanks to the warm summery breeze, I would smell the ume plums and often pinched some to taste!

To make umeboshi or *umeshu* (plum sake), you can use either unripe green plums or ripe orange plums. Personally, I like to use ripened plums for both umeboshi and *umeshu*. Ripened ume has an amazingly sweet aroma that is more fragrant than apricots. However it doesn't have a sweet flavour and it is toxic as well, although the toxic substance will disappear when the plum is pickled or marinated in salt or liqueur.

After washing the ume plum with *shochu* (clear distilled spirit), simply layer it with salt (up to 18% weight of salt to total weight of ume plum) in a container and put a weight on top of it. After several days, *umesu* (plum vinegar) covers the entire fruit. At this stage, if you like red ume plums, you can add red shiso leaves and leave for a week or so. The colour from the leaves will seep into the ume plums to give it a vibrant red colour. When the rainy season is over around mid-July, it's time to dry the pickled plums. Remove ume plums from the container and dry for a day, then return them to the container to stand overnight. Repeat this step again and on the third day, after drying, you can store the plums in a clean container. They will last indefinitely!

Umeboshi are very sour. This sourness comes from citric acid which you will also find in lemon and other citrus fruits. This citric acid is said to be helpful in getting rid of lactic acid from the body and relieving tiredness. This sour taste also whets the appetite when you are tired and lethargic from heat and humidity.

The combination of citric acid and salt gives umeboshi its antibacterial qualities, making it perfect as a filling for onigiri and for packing into lunchboxes. Because of its salty-sour flavour, most people would think that umeboshi is an acidic ingredient. However, it is an alkaline food. If you often eat foods high in sugar and fats, your blood tends to turn acidic. Eating umeboshi every day helps your blood regain its healthy balance, thus keeping your body healthy.

When I was young, I remember having a very bad cough while visiting my grandma. She wrapped crushed leek and umeboshi in a cotton cloth and wrapped the cloth around my neck, telling me to keep it there for several hours. I remember that it was really smelly and odd looking but my cold got better the next day!

Here are more of my grandmother's tips for using umeboshi as a natural cure:

1. For cold and fever, mix umeboshi with granulated sugar in a cup. Pour in hot water and steep. Drinking this tea makes you perspire, making you feel better the next day.
2. For headaches and toothaches, crush umeboshi into a paste and spread on a clean paper or cloth. Rub it on your temple to sooth headaches or on your cheek to sooth toothaches.
3. To cure a hangover, mix crushed umeboshi with hot green tea and sip slowly.
4. For sore throats, gargle diluted *umesu* 5–10 times a day.

Let's Cook Beautiful Rice!

There are many ways of cooking rice but I would like to introduce you to the typical Japanese way of cooking rice. By paying attention to how you cook rice, the grains will turn out shiny and plump and you will be surprised at how sweet and delicious the rice is! Rice is a dried food. In the same manner as dried beans, vegetables and seaweed, it needs to be handled with care when storing and cooking. Here are some tips to cook beautiful rice:

1. It is very important to check the rice grains carefully before washing. Just a few grains of bad rice will affect the taste and appearance of the lot of cooked rice. When you are scooping rice into the pot or rice cooker, make a quick check and discard any discoloured grains.

2. Wash rice gently. All you need is to gently mix the rice by hand. If you apply too much pressure, the rice will crack and will not be able to absorb water evenly.

3. When washing rice, put rice into a large bowl and add enough water to cover. Mix the rice and water several times using your hand and drain.

4. Without adding water, mix rice again with your hand rhythmically in a circular motion 10 times. Rinse rice with water.

5. Repeat this process five times or more until water becomes almost clear.

6. After washing rice, leave it in a colander and cover with a wet cloth for 30 minutes. While the rice is resting, it will absorb water and the grains will swell. You will see that the colour of the rice changes before and after washing. By absorbing water, the volume will increase between 20% and 30%.

7. To cook rice in a rice cooker, measure rice and add equal amounts of water. Put rice into the rice cooker and cook according to the instructions on the cooker.

8. If you are using a clay pot or iron pot, add one and a half times more water than the amount of washed rice. To cook rice in a clay pot or iron pot, put washed rice and water into the pot and put the lid on. Bring to the boil over medium heat. Reduce heat and simmer for 15 minutes. Remove from heat and leave for 10 minutes covered. Remove lid and mix rice gently with a spatula. Cover with a slightly wet cloth and cover with the lid again until ready to use.

9. If you feel the rice is a little stale, add a pinch of sea salt, a piece of dried *kombu* (kelp) or 1 tsp of sake for 400 g (14$^1/_3$ oz) of rice. This will improve the taste of the rice.

Raw rice 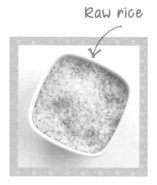 Washed rice  Cooked rice

Things to note before you start:

1. Most of the onigiri in this book weigh 120 g ($4^{1}/_{4}$ oz) unless otherwise mentioned. Feel free to change the size of the onigiri to suit your preferences.

2. Feel free to adjust seasoning according to taste.

3. The recipes in this book are based on easy-to-make portions. For example, cooking 400 ml ($13^{1}/_{2}$ fl oz) of washed rice can yield more than four onigiri. You can freeze the leftover rice for future use.

4. I use Japanese seasoning in this cookbook. They are available at most supermarkets.

5. Use heatproof cling wrap while making onigiri. If you would like to keep onigiri to serve later, leave it to cool before wrapping again in cling wrap and store in a cool and dry place.

Things to note when using the following ingredients:

1. Rice: Japanese short grain rice works best when making onigiri.

2. Salt: Use sea salt as it is more nutritious and tastes milder than refined salt. It will enhance the taste of the rice.

3. Sake: I use sake made for cooking purposes. You can also use regular sake, but make sure to use a neutral-tasting sake. White wine works well too.

4. Sesame seeds: Ready-toasted white and black sesame seeds can be found at most supermarkets. Sesame seeds can also be easily toasted in a non-stick frying pan over low heat.

5. Umeboshi: I use home-made umeboshi in my recipes, but you can easily find umeboshi at Japanese supermarkets.

6. Bonito flakes: Most Japanese branded bonito flakes come in 3 g ($^{1}/_{10}$ oz) and 5 g ($^{1}/_{5}$ oz) packets.

7. Sugar: I use unrefined cane sugar in this cookbook because it is the most natural-tasting.

8. Nori: The size of nori sheets is regulated in Japan and measures 21 x 19-cm ($8^{1}/_{3}$ x $7^{1}/_{2}$-in). For making onigiri, you can use nori sheets that are one-eighth or one-third the size of regular nori sheets, then cut them to your desired size. It's hard to see but the front of the nori sheet is the smooth side.

step one

step two

step three

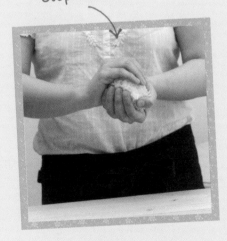

step four

Basic Onigiri

Let's try making basic onigiri using only salt to enjoy the taste of the rice. In this book, I use 120 g (4$^1\!/_2$ oz) cooked rice for a regular-size onigiri and 60 g (2 oz) cooked rice for a small one. This is just an indication. Feel free to change the size of the rice ball according to your preference.

Makes

Cooked Japanese short grain rice (see page 18) 480 g (17 oz)

Water 2 Tbsp

Salt 1 tsp

1. Scoop one portion of cooked rice into a rice bowl. By transferring rice from rice cooker to a bowl, the rice will be cooled down slightly and you will be able to touch the rice without burning your hands. Wet your hands and spread a pinch of salt on your palms and fingers.

2. Transfer rice to your hands.

3. Shape rice into balls or triangles by gently pressing rice 2–3 times with both hands.

4. Adjust the shape of the onigiri if necessary.

Note When you are shaping the rice balls, pressing it 2–3 times is key. If you press too many times, the onigiri will be very hard. However, if you press too lightly, the onigiri will collapse once you bite into it. This process will get easier with practice.

Be careful when you touch hot rice. If the rice is too hot for you to handle, try rolling it in a bowl in a circular motion first before transferring it into your hands. It is better to use freshly cooked rice as it will be stickier and hence easier to handle.

Let's Put Some Filling
in Our Onigiri

Umeboshi, Bonito Flakes and Salmon Onigiri

These three onigiri are very popular in Japan and can be considered Japanese comfort food. In my favourite film, *Kamome Shokudo/Ruokola Lokki* (*Seagull Dinner*), there is a scene in which the girl running the diner says that these three onigiri are "the true onigiri". I agree with this because I never get bored with these ingredients for onigiri! You can easily find umeboshi, bonito flakes and salmon onigiri in supermarkets and convenience stores all over Japan. Umeboshi (pickled plums) is considered a superfood. It has a strong antiseptic effect and is purported to be full of health benefits. In addition, it also prevents rice from going bad. You can read more about the power of umeboshi on page 16.

Makes

Umeboshi onigiri

Cooked Japanese short grain rice (see page 18) 240 g (8½ oz)

Umeboshi 2, medium, pitted

Salt ½ tsp

Nori seaweed sheets 2

Bonito flakes onigiri

Bonito flakes 3 g (1/10 oz)

Japanese soy sauce (shoyu) 2 tsp

Cooked Japanese short grain rice (see page 18) 240 g (8½ oz)

Salt ½ tsp

Nori seaweed sheets 2

Umeboshi onigiri

1. Scoop half the rice into a rice bowl. Make a 2-cm (1-in) indentation in the rice with your finger and put 1 umeboshi in the centre.

2. To form onigiri, wet your hands and spread a pinch of salt on your palms and fingers. Transfer rice to your hands and gently press rice 2–3 times into your preferred shape. Make sure filling is completely covered with rice. Wrap nori around rice ball as desired. Repeat with the remaining ingredients.

Bonito flakes onigiri

1. Mix bonito flakes with soy sauce in a small bowl.

2. Scoop half the rice into a rice bowl. Make a 2-cm (1-in) indentation in the rice with your finger and add a bit of bonito mixture. Continue to form onigiri as above.

Salmon onigiri

Salmon fillet 1, about 70–80 g
   (2$^{1}/_{2}$–3 oz)

Salt 1 tsp + more to taste

**Cooked Japanese short grain
   rice (see page 18)** 240 g
   (8$^{1}/_{2}$ oz)

Nori seaweed sheets 2

Salmon onigiri

1. Season salmon with salt and grill both sides in a frying
pan for a couple of minutes. Remove from heat and remove
skin and bones. Return salmon fillet to pan and cook over
low heat. Use a pair of chopsticks to break salmon into
pieces. Add a pinch of salt and set aside to cool.

2. Scoop half the rice into a rice bowl. Make a 2-cm (1-in)
indentation in the rice with your finger and add some
salmon flakes. Continue to form onigiri as above.

Note There are various types of nori sheets available. For
onigiri, use unseasoned nori. Because nori gets limp fast in
humid weather, keep in an airtight container and store it in
the refrigerator. An easy way to crisp up nori is to run it over
an open flame for a few seconds until it turns dark green
and fragrant.

Tarako Onigiri

Tarako is salted cod roe that can be eaten raw or cooked by grilling or boiling before consumption. Because it has a very short shelf life, eat it as soon as you buy it or store it in the freezer. Some people like well-cooked salted cod roe but I love eating it half-cooked. Besides eating it with onigiri, I love adding *tarako* to pasta or mixing it in mashed potato. The salty-sweet taste and texture of *tarako* is fun and delicious! This onigiri has been my favourite since I was little. When my mother makes this version, she adds a generous amount of roe. Because of this, I've never been happy with other salted cod roe onigiri as I always prefer my mother's!

Makes

Salted cod roe (*tarako*) 100 g
(3^1/$_2$ oz)

**Cooked Japanese short grain
rice (see page 18)** 480 g
(17 oz)

Salt 1 tsp

Nori seaweed sheets 4

1. Place salted cod roe on a sheet of aluminium foil and grill in a toaster oven for 2 minutes. Alternatively, boil a pot of water and cook salted cod roe for 1 minute. Divide salted cod roe into 4 portions.

2. Scoop one-quarter of the rice into a rice bowl. Make a 2-cm (1-in) indentation in the rice with your finger and add some salted cod roe.

3. To form onigiri, wet your hands and spread a pinch of salt on your palms and fingers. Transfer rice to your hands and gently press rice 2–3 times into your preferred shape. Make sure filling is completely covered with rice. Wrap nori around rice ball as desired. Repeat with the remaining ingredients.

Meatball Onigiri

My mother prepared my lunchbox every day for 6 years! My favourite filling was meatball and it always made my lunchbox look very special. For this onigiri, I added some cabbage for a different texture. You can make a big batch of meatballs and freeze them for the next special meatball onigiri day!

Makes

Cooked Japanese short grain rice (see page 18) 400 g (14^1/$_3$ oz)

Cabbage ^{1}/$_8$ head, shredded

Salt 1 tsp

Nori seaweed sheets 4

Meatballs

Onion ^{1}/$_2$, medium, peeled

Carrot 20 g (^{2}/$_3$ oz), peeled

Rosemary leaves (optional) 6

Minced meat (pork and beef half and half) 150 g (5^1/$_3$ oz)

Egg ^{1}/$_2$, medium

Breadcrumbs 1 tsp

Salt a pinch

Ground white pepper a pinch

Milk 1 Tbsp

Potato starch 1 tsp

Vegetable oil 2 Tbsp

Sauce

Water 50 ml (1^2/$_3$ fl oz)

Red wine 50 ml (1^2/$_3$ fl oz)

Sugar 2 tsp

Tomato ketchup 1 Tbsp

Rice vinegar 1 Tbsp

Japanese soy sauce (shoyu) 1 tsp

Worcestershire sauce 1 Tbsp

1. Prepare meatballs. Put onion, carrot, rosemary, minced meat, egg, breadcrumbs, salt, pepper and milk in a food processor and blend to combine. If not using food processor, chop onion, carrot and rosemary very fine and add to meat, breadcrumbs, milk, salt, pepper and egg in a bowl. Mix well with your hands until mixture becomes sticky.

2. Shape mixture into balls measuring about 2-cm (1-in) in diameter. Sprinkle potato starch over meatballs.

3. Heat the oil in a pan and cook meatballs. Set aside.

4. To make sauce, combine water, red wine, sugar, tomato ketchup, rice vinegar, soy sauce and Worcestershire sauce in a small pot and cook over medium heat.

5. When mixture starts to boil, lower the heat. Cook until sauce thickens. Remove from heat.

6. Coat meatballs with sauce and set aside.

7. To form onigiri, scoop one-quarter of rice into a rice bowl. Make a 2-cm (1-in) indentation in the rice with your finger and add some cabbage and 1 meatball.

8. Wet your hands and spread a pinch of salt on your palms and fingers. Transfer rice to your hands and gently press rice 2–3 times into a ball. Make sure the filling is completely covered with rice. Wrap nori around rice ball as desired. Repeat with the remaining ingredients.

Tonkatsu Onigiri

This onigiri is substantial even though only a small amount of rice is used, making it suitable for a hearty lunch. If you have *tonkatsu* left over from a meal, you can use that and it will work just as well. Using store-bought *tonkatsu* sauce can save you some preparation time.

Makes

Cooked Japanese short grain rice (see page 18) 160 g (5²/₃ oz)

Nori seaweed sheets 4

Cabbage ¹/₈ head, shredded

Toasted white sesame seeds to sprinkle

Tonkatsu

Pork loin cutlet 100 g (3¹/₂ oz)

Plain (all-purpose) flour 4 Tbsp

Egg 1, medium, beaten

Breadcrumbs 5 Tbsp

Vegetable oil for deep-frying

Store-bought *tonkatsu* sauce 3 Tbsp

1. To prepare *tonkatsu,* pound the pork loin lightly and cut into 2 x 5-cm (1 x 2-in) sticks. Coat pork with flour, egg and breadcrumbs in this order.

2. Heat oil for deep-frying and cook the pork loin until golden brown. Remove and drain well with kitchen towels.

3. Coat pork loin in *tonkatsu* sauce and set aside.

4. To form onigiri, scoop 40 g (1¹/₄ oz) of rice on a sheet of nori and spread rice evenly.

5. Place a pinch of shredded cabbage in the centre of the rice and top with a piece of pork.

6. Roll nori and rice up into a cone. Garnish with some sesame seeds. Repeat with the remaining ingredients.

Karaage Onigiri

Karaage (Japanese-style deep-fried chicken) is one of the most common items you'll find in a typical Japanese lunchbox. My mother always makes *karaage* with lots of ginger. You can also make a delicious version by adding a pinch of curry powder, powdered almonds or sliced almonds to the batter. You can easily find frozen *karaage* at most supermarkets, but I recommend making it from scratch as it's so easy to do.

Makes

Cooked Japanese short grain rice (see page 18) 400 g (14$^1/_3$ oz)

Salt 1 tsp

Nori seaweed sheets 4

Karaage

Japanese soy sauce (shoyu) 1 Tbsp

Sake 1 Tbsp

Mirin 1 tsp

Ginger 4-cm (1$^1/_2$-in) knob, peeled and grated

Boneless chicken thighs 150 g (5$^1/_3$ oz), cut into bite-size cubes

Potato starch 3 Tbsp

Freshly ground black pepper a pinch

Vegetable oil for deep-frying

1. Prepare *karaage*. Put soy sauce, sake, mirin and ginger in a small bowl and mix well.

2. Add chicken and leave to marinate for 20–30 minutes.

3. Combine potato starch and black pepper in a resealable bag and shake to mix well. Put marinated chicken in the bag and shake the bag to coat the chicken thoroughly. Take chicken out of the bag and shake off any excess potato starch.

4. Heat oil for deep-frying and cook chicken until golden brown and crisp. Drain well on kitchen towels and set aside to cool.

5. To form onigiri, scoop one-quarter of the rice into a rice bowl. Make a 2-cm (1-in) indentation in the rice with your finger and add some deep-fried chicken.

6. Wet your hands and spread a pinch of salt on your palms and fingers. Transfer rice to your hands and gently press rice 2–3 times and shape into a ball. Make sure the filling is completely covered with rice. Wrap nori around rice ball as desired. Repeat with the remaining ingredients.

Note When you prepare the chicken, remove any fat before cooking. The *karaage* will taste good even when it is cold!

Tuna and Mayonnaise Onigiri

Tuna and mayonnaise onigiri is easily found at convenience stores and supermarkets in Japan. If you like wasabi, add a small amount into the tuna mixture. The refreshing taste of wasabi goes really well with tuna and mayonnaise.

1. Combine tuna, mayonnaise and lemon juice in a bowl and mix well. If you like, add a small amount of wasabi to the tuna mixture.

2. Scoop one-quarter of the rice into a rice bowl. Make a 2-cm (1-in) indentation in the rice with your finger and add 1 Tbsp tuna mixture.

3. Wet your hands and spread a pinch of salt on your palms and fingers. Transfer rice to your hands and gently press rice 2–3 times into your preferred shape. Make sure the filling is completely covered with rice. Wrap nori around the rice ball. Repeat with the remaining ingredients.

Note I use Japanese mayonnaise in this book. It contains more vinegar and is less sweet compared to the Western version. I personally think it goes better with Japanese seasoning such as soy sauce and wasabi.

Makes

Canned tuna 4 Tbsp

Mayonnaise 1/2 Tbsp

Lemon juice 1 tsp

Wasabi (optional) to taste

Cooked Japanese short grain rice (see page 18) 480 g (17 oz)

Salt 1 tsp

Nori seaweed sheets 4

Nori Wasabi Onigiri

I love nori and always keep some in my refrigerator. However, it wilts easily when exposed to humidity. When nori sheets become soggy, I often make it into a paste, known as *tsukudani* which can be stored in the refrigerator for up to 2 weeks. *Tsukudani* is a general term for seaweed, seafood and meat simmered with soy sauce, sugar and mirin. The origins of the name come from *Tsukudajima* in Tokyo where *tsukudani* was made for the first time during the Edo period (1603–1868). This nori *tsukudani* is not only tasty with rice, but on toast with butter as well!

1. To make nori paste, put nori and water in a frying pan and bring to the boil over medium heat. Add bonito flakes and cook until most of the moisture evaporates. Add sugar, mirin, sake and soy sauce and cook until mixture thickens, stirring occasionally to mix well. Transfer nori paste to a bowl and leave to cool.

2. Mix 4 Tbsp cooled nori paste with wasabi. Taste and add more wasabi if desired.

3. To form onigiri, scoop one-quarter of the rice into a rice bowl. Make a 2-cm (1-in) indentation in the rice with your finger and add 1 Tbsp nori paste.

4. Wet your hands and spread a pinch of salt on your palms and fingers. Transfer rice to your hands and gently press rice 2–3 times into your preferred shape. Wrap nori around rice ball as desired. Repeat with the remaining ingredients.

Note To make an open style onigiri as shown in the picture, mould the rice and make a shallow indentation in the centre with your finger and add 1 Tbsp of nori paste. Wrap nori around rice ball as desired.

Makes

Wasabi ^{1}/$_3$ tsp + more if needed

Cooked Japanese short grain rice (see page 18) 480 g (17 oz)

Salt 1 tsp

Nori seaweed sheets 4

Nori paste

Nori seaweed sheets 5, 21 x 19-cm (8^1/$_3$ x 7^1/$_2$-in) each, cut into small pieces

Water 200 ml (6^3/$_4$ fl oz)

Bonito flakes 5 g (^{1}/$_5$ oz)

Sugar ^{1}/$_2$ Tbsp

Mirin ^{1}/$_8$ Tbsp

Sake 1 tsp

Japanese soy sauce (shoyu) 1^1/$_2$ Tbsp

Salmon Wasabi Onigiri

Salmon is possibly the most versatile ingredient when it comes to home cooking. You can use it for onigiri, cook it with egg, mix it in a potato salad, use it as a sandwich filling, etc. This onigiri is seasoned with mayonnaise and wasabi. You can omit wasabi if you are not a fan of it. Other variations used for onigiri filling is salmon flakes mixed with avocado and mayonnaise or soy sauce and seven-spice seasoning (*shichimi togarashi*).

Makes

Salmon fillet 1, about 70–80 g (2^1/$_2$–3 oz)

Salt 1 tsp

Mayonnaise 1 tsp

Wasabi ^{1}/$_3$ tsp + more to garnish

Cooked Japanese short grain rice (see page 18) 480 g (17 oz)

Nori seaweed sheets 4

1. Season salmon with salt and grill in a frying pan on both sides for a couple of minutes. Remove from heat and remove skin and bones.

2. Return salmon fillet to the pan and continue to cook over low heat. Use a pair of chopsticks to break salmon into pieces. Add a pinch of salt and set aside to cool.

3. Mix 4 Tbsp salmon flakes with mayonnaise and wasabi. Adjust wasabi and/or salt to taste if necessary.

4. To form onigiri, scoop one-quarter of the rice into a rice bowl. Make a 2-cm (1-in) indentation in the rice with your finger and add 2–3 tsp salmon mixture.

5. Wet your hands and spread a pinch of salt on your palms and fingers. Transfer rice to your hands and gently press rice 2–3 times into your preferred shape. Wrap nori around rice ball and dab some wasabi on top, if desired. Repeat with the remaining ingredients.

Note To make an open style onigiri as shown in the picture, mould the rice and make a shallow indentation in the centre with your finger and add 2 tsp salmon mixture. Wrap nori around rice ball as desired and dab some wasabi on top, if using.

Negi Miso Onigiri

The Japanese leek and miso paste used in this onigiri has a variety of uses. It can be prepared in advance and kept in the refrigerator for up to a week. You can serve this paste simply with rice, topped over grilled deep-fried bean curd *(aburaage)*, as a dip for vegetables or even stir-fried with vegetables and meat. I add quite a lot of ginger to this recipe as it has plenty of health benefits and I love the taste of ginger. The skin of the ginger contains lots of nutrients and flavour. For this recipe, use ginger with the skin intact. And if you can find it, I recommend using organic ginger as it is free from pesticides and chemicals, making the skin safe for consumption.

Makes

Cooked Japanese short grain rice (see page 18) 480 g (17 oz)

Toasted white sesame 1 Tbsp

Salt 1 tsp

Negi-miso paste

Vegetable oil for pan-frying

Japanese leek (*naga negi*) 1, about 80 g (3 oz), finely chopped

Ginger 5-cm (2-in) knob, finely chopped

Miso paste 2 Tbsp

Japanese soy sauce (shoyu) ¹/₂ tsp

Mirin 1 Tbsp

Seven-spice seasoning (*shichimi togarashi*) a dash

Bonito flakes 1 Tbsp

1. Make *negi*-miso paste. Heat oil in a frying pan and sauté leek and ginger until fragrant. Add miso paste, soy sauce and mirin and cook for 2 minutes. Remove from heat. Add seven-spice seasoning and bonito flakes and mix well. Set aside.

2. Scoop rice into a separate bowl and mix in sesame seeds.

3. To form onigiri, scoop one-quarter of the rice mixture into a rice bowl. Make a 2-cm (1-in) indentation in the rice with your finger and add 1 Tbsp *negi*-miso paste.

4. Wet your hands and spread a pinch of salt on your palms and fingers. Transfer rice to your hands and gently press rice 2–3 times into your preferred shape. Repeat with the remaining ingredients.

Note To make an open style onigiri as shown in the picture, mould the rice and make a shallow indentation in the centre with your finger and add 1 Tbsp of negi-miso paste. Wrap nori around rice ball as desired.

Umeboshi Kimchi Onigiri

Umeboshi is a healthy alkaline food and one of the most distinctive Japanese ingredients. This recipe brings together two strong flavours—spicy and sour. The sourness of pickled plums combined with the spiciness of *kimchi* makes this a perfectly balanced onigiri.

Makes

Umeboshi 4, small, pitted

Store-bought *kimchi* 60 g (2 oz), finely chopped

Cooked Japanese short grain rice (see page 18) 480 g (17 oz)

Salt 1 tsp

Toasted white sesame seeds 1 tsp

1. Mince umeboshi with a knife to make a paste. Set aside.

2. Drain *kimchi* by squeezing it with your hands.

3. Mix umeboshi paste and *kimchi* in a small bowl.

4. Scoop one-quarter of the rice into a rice bowl. Make a 2-cm (1-in) indentation in the rice with your finger and add one-quarter of umeboshi-*kimchi* mixture.

5. Wet your hands and spread a pinch of salt on your palms and fingers. Transfer rice to your hands and gently press rice 2–3 times into your preferred shape. Pour sesame seeds on a flat dish and roll rice ball over to coat. Repeat with the remaining ingredients.

Note *Kimchi* is a fermented dish from Korea. It contains a large amount of fibre, vitamins, lactic acid and bacteria. Because it is a fermented food, keep *kimchi* in the refrigerator and make sure to open the container regularly to release built-up gases.

To make an open style onigiri as shown in the picture, mould the rice and roll in sesame seeds, then top with umeboshi-*kimchi* mixture.

Braised Pork Belly Onigiri

Most Japanese families swear by their own version of *buta no kakuni* or braised pork belly—every household has its own special recipe. The key to a delicious dish is in the softness of the pork belly—the best braised pork belly should melt in your mouth.

1. Make braised pork belly. Heat oil in a pot and cook pork belly until slightly browned. Add water and bring to boil. Skim the surface with a slotted spoon to remove any impurities. Add sugar, soy sauce, sake and ginger. Lower heat and cook, covered, for 30 minutes. Remove from heat.

2. To form onigiri, scoop one-quarter of the rice into a bowl. Make a 2-cm (1-in) indentation in the rice with your finger and add 1–2 small pieces of pork belly. Spoon $^{1}/_{4}$ tsp English mustard on top of pork belly.

3. Wet your hands and spread a pinch of salt on your palms and fingers. Transfer rice to your hands and gently press rice 2–3 times into your preferred shape. Make sure that the filling is completely covered with rice. Wrap nori around rice ball as desired and garnish with white radish sprouts. Repeat with the remaining ingredients.

Note To make braised pork belly more substantial for lunch and dinner, add a hard-boiled egg. Simply simmer a peeled hard-boiled egg in the braised pork belly sauce.

Makes

Cooked Japanese short grain rice (see page 18) 400 g (14$^{1}/_{3}$ oz)

English mustard 1 tsp

Salt 1 tsp

Nori seaweed sheets 4

White radish (*daikon*) sprouts to garnish

Braised pork belly

Vegetable oil 2 Tbsp

Pork belly 200 g (7 oz), cut into bite-size pieces

Water 250 ml (8 fl oz / 1 cup)

Sugar 1 Tbsp

Japanese soy sauce (shoyu) 100 ml (3$^{1}/_{3}$ fl oz)

Sake 50 ml (1$^{2}/_{3}$ fl oz)

Ginger 10-cm (5-in) knob, peeled and finely chopped

Makes

Cooked Japanese short grain
rice (see page 18) 480 g
(17 oz)

Salt 1 tsp

Sesame oil for brushing onigiri

Toasted white sesame seeds
4 Tbsp

Nori seaweed sheets 4

Bibimbap

Bean sprouts 60 g (2 oz), tails
plucked

Carrot 30 g (1 oz), peeled and
cut into 2-cm (1-in) lengths

Garlic chives 40 g (1½ oz),
cut into 2-cm (1-in) lengths

Vegetable oil 2 tsp

Minced beef 200 g (7 oz)

Japanese soy sauce (shoyu)
4 Tbsp

Sugar 2 Tbsp

Grated apple or apple juice
2 Tbsp

Minced garlic ½ tsp

Seasoning

Minced garlic ½ tsp

Chicken stock granules ½ tsp

Salt 1 tsp

Freshly ground black pepper
to taste

Sesame oil 2 Tbsp

Bibimbap Onigiri

Bibimbap is a Korean dish that contains plenty of vegetables and spicy chilli paste. I crave this dish when I'm tired. The aroma of sesame oil is so appetising! Feel free to use your favourite vegetables to create your own version of *bibimbap*.

1. Make *bibimbap*. Place bean sprouts, carrot and garlic chives on a heatproof dish and cook in a microwave oven on High for 5 minutes or until soft.

2. Remove from microwave oven and drain the vegetables by squeezing with your hands.

3. Combine seasoning ingredients in a small bowl and mix well. Pour seasoning over the vegetables and mix well. Set aside.

4. Heat vegetable oil in a frying pan and stir-fry minced beef until meat changes colour. Add soy sauce, sugar, grated apple or apple juice and garlic. Mix well. Remove from heat and set aside.

5. To form onigiri, wet your hands and spread a pinch of salt on your palms and fingers. Transfer one-eighth of the rice to your hands and gently press rice 2–3 times into a round patty. You can use a cookie cutter to get an even shape. Repeat this step to make 8 rice patties.

6. Put 1 Tbsp vegetables and 1 Tbsp minced meat on top of a rice patty. Top with another rice patty.

7. Brush some sesame oil on the surface of the rice patty and coat with sesame seeds. Wrap with nori. Repeat with the remaining ingredients.

Let's Mix Rice for
            Our Onigiri

Kinpira Gobou Onigiri

Kinpira gobou, or simmered burdock, is full of fibre. This is a great item for a lunchbox as it goes really well with rice. You can put it into onigiri or layer it between rice patties like a sandwich. *Kinpira gobou* can be kept refrigerated for up to 4 days.

Makes

Cooked Japanese short grain rice (see page 18) 480 g (17 oz)

Toasted black sesame seeds to garnish

Kinpira gobou

Burdock (*gobou*) 100 g (3¹/₂ oz), peeled and shredded

Sake 1¹/₂ Tbsp

Japanese soy sauce (shoyu) 1¹/₂ Tbsp

Sugar ¹/₂ Tbsp

Sesame oil 1 tsp

Japanese chilli pepper (*togarashi*) ¹/₂, about 3-cm (1¹/₂-in), seeded and thinly sliced

Carrot 30 g (1 oz), peeled and shredded

Toasted white sesame seeds to taste

1. **Prepare *kinpira gobou*.** Soak burdock in water for 10 minutes. Drain well.

2. **Combine sake, soy sauce and sugar** in a small bowl and stir to mix well. Set aside.

3. **Heat sesame oil in a frying pan and sauté Japanese chilli pepper.** Add burdock and carrot and cook for 3–4 minutes. When vegetables are soft, pour in soy sauce mixture from the edge of the pan in a circular motion and mix well. When most of the moisture has evaporated, add white sesame seeds and mix well. Remove from heat and set aside to cool.

4. **To form onigiri, put *kinpira gobou* and rice in a bowl and mix well.**

5. **Place cling wrap in a rice bowl and scoop one-quarter of the rice mixture into the bowl.** Pull out rice together with cling wrap and mould rice into a ball. Remove cling wrap and garnish with some black sesame seeds. Repeat with the remaining ingredients.

Note For this recipe, I use thinly shredded burdock and carrot so that they can be mixed well with rice. To make this dish a main course, shred the burdock and carrot into thicker strips so you can enjoy the crunch of the vegetables.

Bonito Flakes and Cheese Onigiri

Bonito flakes and cheese? I know this doesn't sound right but the combination works well! You can serve this bite-size onigiri as a snack to go with drinks. If you like melted cheese, serve this onigiri as soon as you make it. For wasabi lovers, add a little wasabi to the mixture.

1. Combine all the ingredients in a bowl and mix well.

2. Place cling wrap in a rice bowl and scoop 60 g (2 oz) rice mixture into the bowl. Pull out rice together with cling wrap and mould rice into your preferred shape. Repeat with the remaining ingredients.

Makes

Bonito flakes 3 g ($^1/_{10}$ oz)

Japanese soy sauce (shoyu) 2 Tbsp

Mozzarella 120 g ($4^1/_3$ oz), grated

Toasted white sesame seeds 2 Tbsp, ground

Wasabi (optional) to taste

Cooked Japanese short grain rice (see page 18) 480 g (17 oz)

Wakame Seaweed Onigiri

Wakame seaweed contains lots of calcium and minerals and is available dried from most supermarkets all year round. It's funny but I love eating wakame seaweed onigiri in summer. Perhaps it is because the aroma of the seaweed reminds me of the summer breeze!

Makes

Dried wakame seaweed
6 Tbsp

Cooked Japanese short grain rice (see page 18) 480 g (17 oz)

Toasted white sesame seeds
2 Tbsp

Salt to taste

Nori seaweed sheets 4

1. Put dried wakame in a resealable bag and crush with a rolling pin or crumble with your hands. Set aside.

2. Put rice and crushed wakame seaweed in a bowl and mix well. Cover the bowl with a wet cloth. Set aside for 5 minutes.

3. Add sesame seeds to the rice and mix well. Taste and add salt if needed.

4. Place cling wrap in a rice bowl and scoop one-eighth of the rice mixture into the bowl. Pull out rice together with cling wrap and mould rice into your preferred shape. Remove cling wrap and wrap nori around rice ball as desired. Repeat with the remaining ingredients.

Note For a variation on this onigiri, add bonito flakes or chopped umeboshi to the wakame seaweed and mix with rice.

Dried Sakura Ebi and Ginger Onigiri

I love ginger and I always keep a jar of pickled ginger and frozen ginger at home. You will be surprised at how easy it is to grate frozen ginger! I created this recipe when I had some leftover *sakura ebi* (dried sakura shrimps). I use it when I make *okonomiyaki* (flour and cabbage pancake) and there are always leftovers.

Makes

Cooked Japanese short grain
  rice (see page 18) 480 g
  (17 oz)

Pickled sliced ginger (see
  note) 40 g (1^1/$_2$ oz), drained

Dried sakura shrimps
  (*sakura ebi*) 3 Tbsp

Toasted white sesame seeds
  to taste

Japanese soy sauce (shoyu)
  3 Tbsp

White radish (*daikon*)
  sprouts to garnish

1. Put rice, pickled ginger, dried sakura shrimps, sesame seeds and soy sauce in a bowl and mix gently until all the ingredients are well combined.

2. Place cling wrap in a rice bowl and scoop one-eighth of the rice mixture into the bowl. Pull out rice together with cling wrap and mould rice into a triangle or ball. Remove cling wrap and garnish with white radish sprouts. Repeat with the remaining ingredients.

Note Making pickled ginger is very easy. Combine 150 ml (5 fl oz) rice vinegar, 6 Tbsp sugar and ^{1}/$_2$ tsp salt in a clean container and mix well. Add 300–400 g (10^1/$_2$–14^1/$_3$ oz) sliced unpeeled ginger and stir to mix well. Keep in an airtight container in the refrigerator overnight before using. This pickled ginger can be stored in the refrigerator for up to 3 months.

Tenkasu Okaka Onigiri

Ten is from *tenpura* and *kasu* means "rubbish". Yes, now you can imagine what the phrase means. *Tenkasu* is a by-product from preparing tempura. It's the leftover fried batter, which we normally discard. However, in Japan, there are many recipes using *tenkasu*. If you have a nice Japanese tempura restaurant nearby, I'm sure they can give you some or sell it to you cheaply. *Tenkasu* tastes wonderful added to hot noodle dishes. You can also make your own *tenkasu*. When making tempura, sprinkle extra batter into the hot oil to form 0.5–1-cm ($^1/_4$–$^1/_2$-in) round discs. Fry for about 1 minute until the *tenkasu* becomes golden brown and crisp. Remove and drain on kitchen towels. *Tenkasu* can be stored in the refrigerator for up to a week.

1. Combine *tenkasu*, sesame seeds, bonito flakes and soy sauce in a bowl and mix well. Add rice and mix gently until well combined. Add more soy sauce to taste, if desired.

2. Place cling wrap in a rice bowl and scoop one-quarter of the rice into the bowl. Pull out rice together with cling wrap and mould rice into your preferred shape. Remove cling wrap and wrap with nori as desired. Repeat with the remaining ingredients.

Note The mixture of soy sauce and bonito flakes is called *okaka*. Bonito flakes onigiri is known as *okaka* onigiri in Japan.

Makes

Tenkasu 8–10 Tbsp

Toasted white sesame seeds 4 Tbsp

Bonito flakes 12 g ($^2/_5$ oz)

Japanese soy sauce (shoyu) 4 Tbsp + more to taste

Cooked Japanese short grain rice (see page 18) 480 g (17 oz)

Nori seaweed sheets 4

Soboro Onigiri

Soboro literally means "finely crumbled". It can be made from chicken, pork, beef, prawns or eggs and is a great dish to prepare in advance and store. It goes well with rice and onigiri and can be used for a variety of dishes. You can keep *soboro* in an airtight container for up to a week in the refrigerator or a month in the freezer.

Makes

Vegetable oil 1 Tbsp

Minced lean chicken 250 g (9 oz)

Sugar 2 Tbsp

Mirin 2 Tbsp

Japanese soy sauce (shoyu) 3 Tbsp

Sake 25 ml (⁴/₅ fl oz)

Cooked Japanese short grain rice (see page 18) 480 g (17 oz)

Nori seaweed sheets 4

1. To make chicken *soboro*, heat vegetable oil in a frying pan and cook minced chicken. Use a pair of chopsticks to separate the meat into small pieces.

2. Lower heat and add sugar, mirin, soy sauce and sake. Cook until moisture evaporates, about 30 minutes, mixing constantly with chopsticks. Remove from heat and set aside to cool.

3. Combine rice and chicken mixture in a bowl and mix well.

4. Place cling wrap in a rice bowl and scoop one-quarter of the rice mixture into the bowl. Pull out rice together with cling wrap and mould rice into a ball or triangle. Remove cling wrap and wrap rice ball with nori as desired. Repeat with the remaining ingredients.

Edamame Onigiri

Edamame are unripe green soy beans. They are full of nutrients and are easy to prepare. If you can get fresh edamame, try blanching them for a simple but great tasting snack. Edamame can be found in the frozen section at most supermarkets all year round. By seasoning edamame with a good amount of salt, the beans become a great ingredient for onigiri.

Makes

Fresh or frozen edamame
  80 g (3 oz)

Water 500 ml (16 fl oz / 2 cups)

Salt 20 g (²/₃ oz)

Cooked Japanese short grain
  rice (see page 18) 480 g
  (17 oz)

Toasted white sesame seeds
  (optional) 2 Tbsp

1. If using fresh edamame, wash edamame and cut ends of the pods. Sprinkle over a large pinch of salt and mix well. Bring water to the boil and add the remaining salt. Add edamame and boil for 4 minutes. Drain well and set aside to cool.

2. If using frozen edamame, cook according to instructions on the package. If needed, sprinkle a pinch of salt over defrosted edamame.

3. Remove edamame from pods and set aside.

4. To make onigiri, combine rice, edamame and sesame seeds, if using, in a bowl and mix well.

5. Place cling wrap in a rice bowl and scoop one-eighth of the rice mixture into the bowl. Pull out rice together with cling wrap and mould rice into a ball. Repeat with the remaining ingredients.

Myoga and Cucumber Onigiri

Myoga ginger flower buds have a strong fragrance and a slightly bitter flavour. This seasonal ingredient is available only in the summer in Japan. Myoga can be eaten raw, pickled and cooked. It is especially delicious when added to miso soup or layered on top of bean curd. This myoga and cucumber onigiri is a light and refreshing snack, great for enjoying on a hot day.

1. Combine cucumber and a pinch of salt and mix well. Set aside for 5 minutes. Drain cucumber by squeezing well with your hands.

2. Put rice, cucumber, umeboshi paste, myoga ginger flower buds and shiso leaves in a bowl and gently mix until well combined. Taste and add salt if needed.

3. Place cling wrap in a rice bowl and scoop one-quarter of the rice mixture into the bowl. Pull out rice together with cling wrap and mould rice into your preferred shape. Remove cling wrap and sprinkle sesame seeds on top of rice ball. Repeat with the remaining ingredients.

Makes

Japanese cucumbers 2, about 20-cm (8-in), thinly sliced

Salt a pinch + more to taste

Cooked Japanese short grain rice (see page 18) 480 g (17 oz)

Umeboshi 4, medium, pitted and chopped into a paste

Myoga ginger flower buds 2, thinly sliced

Shiso leaves 8, sliced into thin strips

Toasted white sesame seeds to garnish

Lotus Root and Minced Chicken Onigiri

Lotus root adds texture to dishes, whether it is simmered or steamed. This lotus root mixture is a versatile ingredient—you can mix it with rice, add it to omelette or combine it with steamed potato to make croquettes. If you have any leftover lotus root and minced chicken mixture after making this onigiri, you can keep it in the refrigerator for up to 4 days. I often save leftover lotus root dishes to include in lunchboxes.

Makes

Lotus root 200 g (7 oz), peeled and cut into 0.5-cm (1/4-in) cubes

Water 500 ml (16 fl oz / 2 cups)

Rice vinegar 1 tsp

Sugar 1 Tbsp

Japanese soy sauce (shoyu) 3 Tbsp

Mirin 2 Tbsp

Grated ginger 2 tsp

Minced chicken 200 g (7 oz)

Cooked Japanese short grain rice (see page 18) 480 g (17 oz)

1. Soak lotus root in water and vinegar to prevent discolouration. Set aside for 5–10 minutes. Rinse in cold running water and drain well. Set aside.

2. Combine sugar, soy sauce, mirin and ginger in a small bowl. Mix well.

3. Heat a frying pan and cook minced meat until the colour changes. Add lotus root and cook until transparent. Add the soy sauce mixture and mix well. Cook until moisture has evaporated. Remove from heat and set aside to cool.

4. Put rice into a bowl and add 8–10 Tbsp lotus root and chicken mixture. Mix well.

5. Place cling wrap in a rice bowl and scoop one-quarter of the rice mixture into the bowl. Pull out rice together with cling wrap and mould rice into your preferred shape. Repeat with the remaining ingredients.

Gapao Onigiri

Gapao kai kao is a Thai rice dish made with minced meat and Thai basil. It is very spicy and flavourful. I love this dish and it is my inspiration for this onigiri.

Makes

Vegetable oil 2 Tbsp + 2 tsp

Minced garlic 1 Tbsp

Japanese red chilli (*togarashi*)
$1/2$–1, according to taste, seeded and thinly sliced

Minced chicken 150 g
($5^1/_3$ oz)

Minced pork 150 g ($5^1/_3$ oz)

Japanese green pepper
(*piman*) 5, seeded and chopped

Thai basil or basil 20 leaves, chopped + more for garnishing

Cooked Japanese short grain rice (see page 18) 400 g
($14^1/_3$ oz)

Seasoning

Fish sauce 1 Tbsp

Oyster sauce 5 Tbsp

Japanese soy sauce (shoyu)
2 tsp

Sugar 2 tsp

Sake 2 tsp

Egg crêpe

Eggs 4

Milk 4 Tbsp

Potato starch 4 tsp

1. Combine seasoning ingredients in a small bowl and mix well.

2. Heat 2 Tbsp oil in a frying pan and sauté garlic and Japanese red chilli until fragrant. Add minced chicken and pork and cook until meat changes colour. Add green pepper and fry for 1 minute. Add seasoning ingredients and stir well. Remove from heat and add basil leaves. Mix well and set aside.

3. Meanwhile, combine eggs, milk and potato starch in a small bowl and mix well.

4. Heat some oil in a clean frying pan and pour in one-quarter of the egg mixture. Swirl the egg mixture in the pan to form a thin crêpe about 15-cm (6-in) in diameter. Cook both sides and set aside. Repeat this process until the egg mixture is used up. You should have 4 egg crêpes.

5. To make onigiri, combine rice and 6–7 Tbsp minced meat mixture in a bowl and mix well. Taste rice and add more salt if needed.

6. Place cling wrap in a rice bowl and scoop one-quarter of the rice mixture into the bowl. Pull out rice together with cling wrap and mould rice into your preferred shape. Remove cling wrap and carefully wrap rice ball with an egg crêpe, sit the rice ball on the ends of crêpe. Make a cut on the top of the crêpe so the rice ball is exposed. Garnish with basil leaves. Repeat with the remaining ingredients.

Shiso Leaf and Salmon Onigiri

This colourful onigiri is aromatic thanks to the inclusion of shiso leaves and sesame seeds. In Japan, shiso leaves are a favourite ingredient in the summer. Even if you don't feel like eating, the fresh aroma from the shiso leaves will whet your appetite.

Makes

Japanese cucumber 2, about 20-cm (8-in) each, thinly sliced

Salt a pinch + more to taste

Cooked Japanese short grain rice (see page 18) 480 g (17 oz)

Shiso leaves 8, thinly sliced

Toasted white sesame seeds 4 Tbsp

Salmon (see page 24) 8 Tbsp, flaked

1. Combine cucumber and a pinch of salt in a bowl and mix well. Set aside for 5 minutes. Drain cucumber by squeezing well with your hands.

2. Put rice, shiso leaves, sesame seeds, salmon flakes and cucumber in a large bowl and mix well. Taste and add more salt if needed.

3. Place cling wrap in a rice bowl and scoop one-quarter of the rice into the bowl. Pull out rice together with cling wrap and mould rice into your preferred shape. Repeat with the remaining ingredients.

Garlic Bacon Onigiri

Crispy bacon and soft rice gives this onigiri a wonderful contrast of textures. It goes well with onion or chicken soup. Mixing it with a large pinch of black pepper will make this onigiri perfect for pairing with beer!

1. Put olive oil and garlic in a frying pan and turn on the heat. Cook until garlic is fragrant, then add bacon and sauté until bacon is crisp. Season with salt and pepper. Remove from heat and drain well.

2. Combine rice, bacon and chives in a bowl and mix well. Place cling wrap in a rice bowl and scoop one-eighth of the rice mixture into bowl. Pull out rice together with cling wrap and mould rice into your preferred shape. Repeat with the remaining ingredients.

Makes

Olive oil 2 tsp

Garlic 2 cloves, peeled and finely chopped

Bacon 4 rashers, finely chopped

Salt to taste

Freshly ground black pepper to taste

Cooked Japanese short grain rice (see page 18) 480 g (17 oz), cooled

Chopped chives 1–2 Tbsp

Nameshi Onigiri

White radish (*daikon*) leaves are not only delicious, they are also full of calcium, vitamin C and beta-carotene. It used to be easier to find white radish with leaves still attached at the supermarkets, but the leaves are now trimmed to extend the shelf life of the radish. However, it is very easy to grow white radish leaves at home. Simply cut off the top of a white radish and soak it in water. Beautiful green leaves will appear in several days! You can use these leaves in miso soup or mix them with rice as with this recipe.

Makes

Salt a pinch + $^1/_2$ tsp

White radish (*daikon*) leaves 200 g (7 oz)

Cooked Japanese short grain rice (see page 18) 480 g (17 oz), cooled

Toasted white sesame seeds 2 tsp

1. Boil a pot of water and add a pinch of salt. Blanch white radish leaves for about 1 minute. Immediately plunge leaves in iced water to stop it from cooking further. Drain leaves by patting dry with kitchen towels.

2. Chop leaves into 0.5-cm ($^1/_4$-in) lengths and place in a bowl. Sprinkle $^1/_2$ tsp salt over the leaves and mix well. Add rice and sesame seeds and mix well. Taste and add more salt if needed.

3. Place cling wrap in a rice bowl and scoop one-quarter of the rice into the bowl. Pull out rice together with cling wrap and mould rice into your preferred shape. Repeat with the remaining ingredients.

Goya Chanpuru Onigiri

Goya is bittergourd in Japanese and *chanpuru* is a form of stir-fried dish. *Goya chanpuru* is one of Okinawa's most famous dishes and it has become popular throughout Japan. Summer in Japan is very hot and many people lose their appetites. It is said that the bitterness of *goya* whets the appetite and that it has medicinal qualities to energise the body during the hot summer months. When I first ate *goya*, I was surprised by its harsh bitterness, but now I'm addicted to it!

1. Cut bittergourd into half lengthwise and remove seeds. Cut the bittergourd again in half lengthwise, then slice thinly.

2. Place bittergourd into a bowl and add a pinch of salt. Mix well. Leave aside for 3–5 minutes. Taste and if bittergourd is too bitter, leave for another 1 minute. Rinse in cold water and drain well by squeezing with your hands.

3. Combine seasoning ingredients in a small container and mix well.

4. Heat oil in a large frying pan and stir-fry luncheon meat or ham until slightly browned. Add bittergourd, pepper and seasoning ingredients. Stir-fry for a few seconds. Add egg and mix well. Cook until bittergourd is softened and moisture has evaporated. Remove from heat.

5. Combine 6–7 Tbsp bittergourd mixture, bonito flakes and rice in a bowl and mix well. You can add more bittergourd mixture if you like, but adding too much makes it difficult for the rice to stay together.

6. Place cling wrap in a rice bowl and scoop one-quarter of the rice into the bowl. Pull out rice together with cling wrap and mould rice into your preferred shape. Remove cling wrap and garnish with more bonito flakes. Repeat with the remaining ingredients.

Note I use Japanese bittergourd in this recipe. It is small and spiky and more bitter than the long and smooth variety typically used in Chinese and South East Asian cooking. If you can't find Japanese bittergourd or if it is not to your taste, substitute it with the larger variety.

Makes

Japanese bittergourds (*goya*) 20-cm (8-in) each

Salt a pinch + more to taste

Vegetable oil 1 Tbsp

Luncheon meat or ham 120 g (4$^{1}/_{4}$ oz), cut into 0.5–1-cm ($^{1}/_{4}$–$^{1}/_{2}$-in) cubes

Freshly ground black pepper to taste

Egg 1, beaten

Bonito flakes 6 g ($^{1}/_{5}$ oz) + more to garnish

Cooked Japanese short grain rice (see page 18) 480 g (17 oz)

Seasoning

Chicken stock granules 2 tsp

Sake 2 Tbsp

Sesame oil to taste

Japanese soy sauce (shoyu) 2 tsp

Hijiki Onigiri

I never run out of hijiki seaweed at home—it's easy to cook and store. I cook a lot at once and freeze it in silicone cups (15–20 g ($^1/_2$–$^2/_3$ oz) per cup) so that I can pop one cup into a lunchbox or defrost to mix with rice to make onigiri! There are long and short versions of hijiki seaweed at the supermarket but you can cook both in the same way. I'm using the short variety in this recipe as it is easier to mix with rice.

Makes

Dried hijiki seaweed 10 g
($^1/_3$ oz), soaked in water for
30 minutes

Carrot 60 g (2 oz), peeled

Deep-fried bean curd
(aburaage) 1, about 60 g
(2 oz)

Vegetable oil 2 tsp

Water 200 ml (6$^3/_4$ fl oz)

Instant dashi powder
1$^1/_2$ Tbsp

Japanese soy sauce (shoyu)
2 Tbsp

Mirin 2 Tbsp

Cooked Japanese short grain
rice (see page 18) 480 g
(17 oz)

1. Rinse hijiki seaweed and drain well. Set aside.

2. Cut carrot into half lengthwise and then cut again in half lengthwise. Slice thinly.

3. Pour hot water over deep-fried bean curd and drain well, then dry further using kitchen towels. Cut into 2-cm (1-in) strips.

4. Heat oil in a frying pan and sauté hijiki seaweed, carrot and bean curd strips for 1 minute. Add water, instant dashi powder, soy sauce and mirin and cook until moisture is almost evaporated. Remove from heat.

5. Combine 4–5 Tbsp hijiki seaweed mixture and rice in a bowl and mix well.

6. Place cling wrap in a rice bowl and scoop one-quarter of the rice into the bowl. Pull out rice together with cling wrap and mould rice into your preferred shape. Repeat with the remaining ingredients.

Let's Decorate
Our Onigiri

Simple Miso Onigiri

Whenever there is leftover rice, my mother would make this onigiri and leave it on a plate on the dining table. Within several hours, they will all be gone. To make miso onigiri, all you have to do is spread miso paste all over the rice ball—it is as simple as that! I would recommend using *awase* miso which is a combination of red and white miso. White miso is too sweet and dark red miso is too rich so combining them makes a perfect miso. You can enjoy the natural taste of miso paste and the sweetness of the rice in this onigiri. Eating this onigiri hot or cold is equally delicious!

Makes

Cooked Japanese short grain
   rice (see page 18) 480 g
   (17 oz)

Salt a pinch

Miso paste 4 Tbsp

1. Wet your hands and spread a pinch of salt on your fingers and palms. Take one-quarter of the rice in your hands and mould rice 2–3 times into your preferred shape.

2. Spread 1 Tbsp miso paste all over the rice ball. Repeat with the remaining ingredients.

Furikake Onigiri

Japanese rice seasoning powder (*furikake*) is available at most supermarkets. There are many kinds of *furikake*, so choose your favourite and incorporate it into your onigiri. This is a colourful, nutritious and quick snack to prepare!

Makes

Cooked Japanese short grain rice (see page 18) 480 g (17 oz)

Japanese rice seasoning (*furikake*) 8 Tbsp

1. Place cling wrap in a rice bowl and scoop one-eighth of the rice into the bowl. Pull out rice together with cling wrap and mould rice into your preferred shape.

2. Pour *furikake* powder onto a flat dish. Remove cling wrap and roll rice balls over *furikake* powder to coat evenly. Repeat with the remaining ingredients.

Note If you like, you can mix *furikake* powder into rice and make onigiri. You can also add a filling, such as umeboshi, salmon flakes or pickles and sprinkle over with *furikake* powder. It'll be your original onigiri!

Grilled Beef Onigiri

If you are a meat lover, this onigiri is perfect for you. It's so simple yet it can be served as a main dish for lunch or dinner. I use thinly sliced leek as a garnish but chopped spring onion (scallion) or ginger goes well with beef too. If you prefer pork, choose cuts with less fat. This onigiri is great for packing in a lunchbox as it tastes great even when cold.

Makes

Cooked Japanese short grain rice (see page 18) 400 g (14$^{1}/_{3}$ oz)

Toasted sesame seeds 1 Tbsp + more to garnish

Thinly sliced beef 300 g (10$^{1}/_{2}$ oz)

Vegetable oil 2 tsp

Thinly sliced leek to garnish

Seasoning

Japanese soy sauce (shoyu) 4 Tbsp

Sugar 2 Tbsp

Sake 3 Tbsp

Water 4 Tbsp

1. Mix rice and sesame seeds in a bowl. Wet your hands and take one-quarter of the rice and mould into a barrel shape. Repeat with the remaining rice. Set aside to cool.

2. Combine ingredients for seasoning in a small bowl and mix well.

3. Wrap beef around the rice balls.

4. Heat oil in a frying pan and put beef wrapped rice balls into the pan. Make sure the ends of the beef face down. Cook all sides of the beef. Remove from heat and set aside.

5. Add seasoning to the same pan and bring to the boil. Return rice balls to the pan and coat well with the seasoning.

6. Remove from pan and place on a serving plate. Garnish with sesame seeds and thinly sliced leek.

Note For this onigiri, make the rice balls with firmer pressure and wrap beef or pork tightly to prevent the rice from falling apart while grilling.

Tenmusu

Tenmusu originated from the Mie prefecture located in central Japan but is now considered a speciality of Nagoya city. *Ten* is from *tenpura* and *musu* is from *omusubi*. You can also use leftover tempura in this recipe.

Makes

Medium prawns (shrimps) 8

Vegetable oil for deep-frying

Cooked Japanese short grain
    rice (see page 18) 480 g
    (17 oz)

Salt 1 tsp

Nori seaweed sheets 8

Seasoning

Sake 2 Tbsp

Mirin 3 Tbsp

Sugar 2 tsp

Japanese soy sauce (shoyu)
    6 Tbsp

Bonito flakes 3 g ($^1/_{10}$ oz)

Tempura batter

Water 80 g (3 oz)

Sake 1 Tbsp

Ice cubes 2

Plain (all-purpose) flour 50 g
    ($1^2/_3$ oz)

Baking powder $^1/_2$ tsp

1. Prepare seasoning first. Combine sake and mirin in a small pan and bring to the boil. Add sugar, soy sauce and bonito flakes and remove from heat.

2. Prepare prawns. Remove shells and heads but leave the tails intact, then devein. Pat prawns dry with kitchen towels.

3. Prepare tempura batter. Combine water, sake, ice cubes, flour and baking powder in a bowl and mix with a pair of chopsticks in a circular motion 5 times.

4. Heat oil for deep-frying. When the oil reaches 180°C (350°F), dip prawns into batter and deep-fry until golden brown. Drain well. Immediately dip prawns into seasoning sauce and set aside.

5. To form onigiri, scoop one-eighth of the rice into a bowl. Make a 4-cm ($1^1/_2$-in) indentation in the rice with your finger and add a prawn.

6. Wet your hands and spread a pinch of salt on your palms and fingers. Transfer rice to your hands and gently press rice 2–3 times into a triangle. Make sure the rice covers the prawn but leave the tail sticking out. Wrap nori around rice ball. Repeat with the remaining ingredients.

Smoked Salmon Onigiri

This onigiri almost looks like sushi, making it perfect to serve at parties and special events. When using smoked salmon, it's important to serve it as soon as it is prepared.

Makes

Smoked salmon 8 slices, about 5 x 5-cm (2 x 2-in)

Shiso leaves 8

Salt 1 tsp

Cooked Japanese short grain rice (see page 18) 480 g (17 oz)

Lemon 1/4, thinly sliced and cut into triangles

1. Place salmon in the middle of a sheet of cling wrap and put a piece of shiso leaf face down over the salmon.

2. Place cling wrap in a rice bowl and scoop one-eighth of the rice into the bowl. Pull out rice together with cling wrap and mould rice into a ball.

3. Remove cling wrap and garnish rice ball with lemon. Repeat with the remaining ingredients.

Potato Chips and Black Pepper Onigiri

This onigiri is perfect for entertaining at home. You can use your favourite potato chips. This is an easy and tasty onigiri that will appeal to children and beer-drinkers in equal measure!

Makes

Salt 1 tsp

Cooked Japanese short grain rice (see page 18) 480 g (17 oz)

Potato chips as desired

Freshly ground black pepper 1 tsp

1. Mix salt and rice in a bowl.

2. Place cling wrap in a rice bowl and scoop one-eighth of the rice into the bowl. Pull out rice together with cling wrap and mould rice into a ball. Repeat with the remaining ingredients.

3. Crush potato chips and put them on a flat dish. Sprinkle black pepper over the chips and mix well.

4. Remove cling wrap and roll the rice balls on the potato chips to cover completely. Serve immediately.

Omurice Onigiri

Omurice, or Japanese omelette rice, is a popular dish with children. Adding a pinch of Worcestershire sauce makes this onigiri tasty even when it's cold. I'm sure children who don't like vegetables will be happy to eat this onigiri. This is the kind of onigiri I like to pack for a picnic!

Makes

Vegetable oil for shallow-frying

Onion 1/2, peeled and chopped

Chicken breast fillets 1, about 200 g (7 oz) each, pounded and cut into bite-size cubes

Frozen mixed vegetables 50 g (1²/₃ oz)

Sausages 2, cut into small cubes

Cooked Japanese short grain rice (see page 18) 480 g (17 oz)

Seasoning

Worcestershire sauce 1 tsp

Chicken stock granules 2 tsp

Garlic 1/2 clove, peeled and crushed

Salt a pinch

Ground white pepper a pinch

Tomato ketchup 2 Tbsp + more to decorate

Egg crêpe

Eggs 4

Milk 4 Tbsp

Potato starch 4 tsp

Vegetable oil for cooking

1. Combine seasoning ingredients in a small bowl and mix well. Set aside.

2. Heat oil for shallow-frying in a pan and cook onion and chicken until meat changes colour. Remove from pan and set aside.

3. In the same pan, add mixed vegetables and sausage and cook for 1–2 minutes.

4. Add rice and mix well. Add cooked onion and chicken mixture and seasoning ingredients. Mix well. Remove from heat and transfer rice mixture to a plate and set aside.

5. Prepare egg crêpe. Mix eggs, milk and potato starch in a small bowl and stir to mix well.

6. Heat oil in a small clean pan and pour in egg mixture. Swirl the egg mixture around the pan to make a thin crêpe. Cook both sides and set aside. Repeat this process until the egg mixture is used up. Set aside.

7. Place cling wrap in a rice bowl and scoop one-eighth of the rice into the bowl. Pull out rice together with cling wrap and mould rice into your preferred shape. Repeat with the remaining rice.

8. Cut egg sheets into 8 rectangular strips measuring about 15 x 2.5-cm (6 x 1-in). To make a pattern on the egg, use drinking straws to cut out small holes.

9. Remove cling wrap from rice and carefully wrap egg strips around rice balls. Decorate with tomato ketchup, if desired.

SPAM Onigiri

SPAM (or luncheon meat) onigiri is a popular snack in Okinawa. In recent years, however, you can find this onigiri in almost all convenience stores in Japan. Generally luncheon meat contains a large amount of salt, so I recommend that you boil it in water before eating. Both teriyaki sauce and *tonkatsu* sauce go really well with this onigiri. I have included a simple and quick teriyaki sauce with this recipe. You can use this sauce when sautéing chicken, fish and fermented soy beans (*tempeh*).

1. Mix all the ingredients for teriyaki sauce in a small bowl. Set aside.

2. Bring some water to the boil in a frying pan and cook luncheon meat for 2 minutes to get rid of saltiness in the luncheon meat. Discard water and pan-fry luncheon meat without adding oil until brown on both sides.

3. Pour teriyaki sauce over luncheon meat and cook until the sauce thickens. Remove from heat and set aside to cool.

4. Wet your hands and take one-eighth of the rice and shape to match with luncheon meat shape.

5. Place 1 piece of luncheon meat on top of the rice. Wrap rice and luncheon meat with a strip of nori to form a bundle. Garnish with white radish sprouts. Repeat with the remaining ingredients.

Note If you like spicy food, you can mix some freshly ground black pepper into the rice.

Makes

Luncheon meat 100–120 g (3^1/$_2$–4^1/$_4$ oz), cut into 4 slices, about 1-cm (^{1}/$_2$-in) thick, then cut into your preferred shape

Cooked Japanese short grain rice (see page 18) 480 g (17 oz)

Freshly grounded black pepper ^{1}/$_2$ tsp

Nori seaweed sheets 4, cut into 2 x 10-cm (1 x 4-in) strips

White radish (*daikon*) sprouts to garnish

Teriyaki sauce

Japanese soy sauce (shoyu) 4 Tbsp

Sugar 4 Tbsp

Sake 3 Tbsp

Botamochi

I often visited my grandma in August during the summer vacation when I was little. We also celebrated the *obon* holidays during this time and she would always prepare *botamochi* as an offering to our ancestors. *Botamochi* is known by different names at different times of the year. During the spring equinox, it is called *botamochi*; during the autumn equinox, it is called *ohagi*. This sweet rice ball is usually made from glutinous rice, however, I've used Japanese short grain rice in this recipe as it is quicker to prepare.

Makes

Japanese red beans (*adzuki*) 100 g (3¹/₂ oz)

Water as needed

Sugar 100 g (3¹/₂ oz)

Salt ¹/₂ tsp

Red bean paste botamochi
Cooked Japanese short grain rice (see page 18) 200 g (7 oz)

Soy bean powder botamochi

Soy bean powder (*kinako*) 6 Tbsp

Sugar 4 Tbsp

Cooked Japanese short grain rice (see page 18) 200 g (7 oz)

1. Start by preparing red bean paste. Put red beans in a pot and add enough water to cover red beans. Bring to the boil. Once water is boiling, remove from heat and drain. Add the same amount of water and bring to the boil again. Once water is boiling, lower heat and simmer for 40 minutes.

2. While red beans are cooking, use a spoon to skim off any foam that forms on the surface. Check the water level often and add more water as necessary. Do not allow the beans to dry up or burn. To check if the beans are cooked, pinch a few from the pot and press with your fingers. They should be soft and easily crushed. Drain and return red beans to the pot and add sugar. Cook over low heat, stirring constantly until paste is shiny and thick. Remove from heat, add salt and mix well, making sure not to crush the beans. Transfer to a large bowl to cool.

3. To make red bean botamochi, place cling wrap in a rice bowl and scoop half of the rice into the bowl. Pull out rice together with cling wrap and mould rice into a ball.

4. On another sheet of cling wrap, spoon some red bean paste on top and shape the red bean paste into a 10-cm (4-in) patty.

5. Remove cling wrap from rice ball and place rice ball on top of red bean patty. Gradually mould the red beans over the rice ball until it is completely covered. Repeat with the remaining ingredients.

6. To make soy bean powder botamochi, mix soy bean powder and sugar in a small flat container. Set aside.

7. Place cling wrap in a rice bowl and scoop half of the rice into the bowl. Make a 2-cm (1-in) indentation in the rice with your finger and add 1 heaped tsp red bean paste. Cover with more rice.

8. Gently shape rice into a ball. Remove cling wrap and roll the rice ball over the soy bean powder mixture to coat evenly. Repeat with the remaining ingredients.

Niko Niko Onigiri

I name these *niko niko* (smiley) onigiri because they make everyone smile! These onigiri are popular with kids as they can have fun with their food. This is also a great way to introduce foods to kids who are finicky with what they eat! Nori cutters are available from some speciality Japanese stores and on the Internet. There is a variety of cute cut-outs to create many faces easily using nori sheets. I've used linguine to attach the ears to these *niko niko* onigiri. The linguine will soften and can be eaten with the onigiri but feel free to omit it if desired.

Makes

Bear

Cooked Japanese short grain rice (see page 18) 80 g (3 oz)

Japanese soy sauce (shoyu) 1 tsp

Uncooked linguine 1, cut into 4-cm (1¹/₂-in) length

Nori seaweed sheet 1

Tomato ketchup as needed

1. To make bear onigiri, combine rice and soy sauce in a small bowl and mix well.

2. Make 2 rice balls measuring 1-cm (¹/₂-in) in diameter for ears.

3. Place the remaining rice mixture on a sheet of cling wrap. Shape it into a ball to make the face of the bear. Remove cling wrap.

4. Stick a piece of pasta halfway through the small rice balls as joints and attach these to the larger rice ball.

5. Cut eyes, nose and a mouth out of nori using kitchen scissors. Arrange the eyes, nose and mouth of the bear on the larger rice ball. Use a toothpick to dab on rosy ketchup cheeks.

Rabbit

Quail eggs 2

Cooked Japanese short grain rice (see page 18) 80 g (3 oz)

Uncooked linguine 2, cut into 4-cm (1¹/₂-in) length

Ham 1 slice, cut into 5-cm (2-in) rounds

Nori seaweed sheet 1

Tomato ketchup as needed

1. To make rabbit onigiri, boil quail eggs and shell. While eggs are still warm, wrap them individually in cling wrap and roll them into logs to make the ears of the rabbit. Set aside to cool.

2. Place rice on a sheet of cling wrap. Shape it into a ball to make the face for the rabbit. Remove cling wrap.

3. Stick a piece of pasta halfway through each quail egg and attach these to the rice ball.

4. Cut out two 1-cm (¹/₂-in) strips from the ham and place these on the quail eggs to make ears for the rabbit.

5. Cut eyes, nose and mouth out of nori sheet using kitchen scissors. Arrange them on the rice ball. Use a toothpick to dab on rosy ketchup cheeks.

Lion

Egg 1

Milk 1 Tbsp

Potato starch 1 tsp

Vegetable oil 1 Tbsp

Cooked Japanese short grain
  rice (see page 18) 80 g
  (3 oz)

Tomato ketchup 1 Tbsp

Uncooked linguine 1, cut into
  4-cm (1^1/$_2$-in) length

Nori seaweed sheet 1

Sliced cheese 1

Toasted black sesame seeds
  a few

1. To make lion onigiri, beat egg, milk and potato starch in a small bowl.

2. Heat oil in a medium pan (at least 15-cm (6-in) diameter) and pour in egg mixture to create a very thin crêpe. When egg is set, flip it over and cook for another 30 seconds. Remove from heat and set aside to cool.

3. Combine rice and ketchup in a small bowl and mix well.

4. Make 2 rice balls measuring 1-cm (^{1}/$_2$-in) in diameter for ears.

5. Place the remaining rice mixture on a sheet of cling wrap. Shape it into a ball and flatten the sides slightly. Remove cling wrap.

6. To make lion's mane, cut the egg crêpe into a rectangle measuring 15 x 6-cm (6 x 2^1/$_3$-in) and fold it in half lengthwise to get a long rectangle. Cut slits along the folded edge, then fit crêpe into a muffin cup with the folded edge sticking out to resemble a lion's mane.

7. Place large rice ball in the centre of the muffin cup for the lion's face. Stick linguine into small rice balls and attach to the large rice ball.

8. Cut eyes and whiskers out of nori sheet using kitchen scissors. Cut 2 small circles from sliced cheese. Arrange on the rice ball and top with some sesame seeds for the muzzle.

Chick

Cooked Japanese short grain
  rice (see page 18) 80 g
  (3 oz)

Egg 1

Milk 1 Tbsp

Potato starch 1 tsp

Vegetable oil 1 Tbsp

Carrot ^{1}/$_4$, cut several sizes
  for beak and feet

Nori seaweed sheet 1

1. To make chick onigiri, place rice on a sheet of cling wrap. Shape it into an egg. Set aside.

2. Beat egg, milk and potato starch in a small bowl. Heat oil in a pan and pour in two-thirds of the egg mixture. Swirl the pan around to create a thin crêpe measuring about 15-cm (6-in) in diameter. When the egg is set, flip it over and cook for another 30 seconds.

3. Transfer the egg to a cutting board and cut slits measuring about 2-cm (1-in) along the edge of the egg crêpe.

4. Place the egg on a sheet of cling wrap. Remove cling wrap and place rice ball in the centre of the egg.

5. Wrap the rice ball with the egg followed by cling wrap and leave for 5 minutes to mould egg around rice ball. Remove cling wrap.

6. Heat some oil in the pan again and pour in the remaining egg mixture. Move the pan around to create a thin crêpe. Remove from the heat and cut out wings for the chick using kitchen scissors.

7. Cut nose and feet out of carrot and cut eyes out of nori sheet. Arrange wings, nose, feet and eyes on the rice ball.

Photograph on pages 94–95

Let's Grill
Our Onigiri

Soy Sauce and Miso Yaki Onigiri

You can make a delicious grilled (*yaki*) onigiri simply by spreading soy sauce or miso paste over the rice ball and putting it under the grill. The smell of grilled rice is so appealing! There is a whole array of miso pastes available at the supermarket—red or white, with or without grain, rice or wheat. The differences depend on where they are made and what they are made from. People in the Kanto area, including Tokyo, use *aka* miso (red miso) while people in the Kansai region, including Osaka and Kyoto, use *shiro* miso (sweet white miso). Folks in the Tokai area, including Sendai, prefer to use *hatchomiso* (dark brown miso). If you are not familiar with cooking with miso, you can start by using *awase* miso, which is made of 50% white and 50% red miso.

Makes

Grilled soy sauce onigiri
Cooked Japanese short grain rice (see page 18) 240 g (8¹/₂ oz)

Japanese soy sauce (shoyu) 1 Tbsp + more for brushing

Grilled miso onigiri
Cooked Japanese short grain rice (see page 18) 240 g (8¹/₂ oz)

Chopped Japanese leek (*naga negi*) 2 Tbsp

Miso paste 2 Tbsp

Note For another delicious version of soy sauce *yaki* onigiri, sprinkle seven-spice seasoning (*shichimi togarashi*) over the rice ball before brushing with soy sauce and grilling.

1. To make grilled soy sauce onigiri, combine rice and soy sauce in a large bowl and mix well.

2. Scoop one-quarter of the rice mixture into a rice bowl. Wet your hands and transfer rice to your hands. Shape rice into a ball or triangle. Repeat with the remaining rice to make 4 rice balls. Leave rice balls on a plate to cool.

3. Place rice balls on a sheet of aluminium foil and grill in a toaster oven or frying pan until brown on both sides.

4. Brush soy sauce on both sides and grill for another 10 seconds on each side.

5. For grilled miso onigiri, combine rice, leek and miso paste in a small bowl and mix well.

6. Scoop one-quarter of the rice mixture into a rice bowl. Wet your hands and transfer rice to your hands. Shape rice into a ball or triangle. Repeat with the remaining rice to make 4 rice balls. Leave rice balls on a plate to cool.

7. Grill rice balls in an oven toaster or frying pan until brown on both sides.

8. Spread miso paste on 1 side of each rice ball and grill the rice balls with miso paste side down for another 10 seconds. Serve hot.

Goma-miso Chicken Yaki Onigiri

Roasted sesame has a beautiful aroma that whets the appetite. The sauce used in this recipe is very useful—you can use it as a dip for vegetables; stir-fry it with minced meat or layer it over fresh bean curd. Store this *goma*-miso sauce in an airtight container in the refrigerator for up to 4 days.

1. Start by preparing goma-miso sauce. Combine all the ingredients for sauce in a small bowl and stir to mix well.

2. Cut chicken into 2-cm (1-in) cubes. Season chicken with salt and pepper.

3. Heat oil in a frying pan and grill chicken until brown. Add sake and cover pan. Cook for 1 minute.

4. Remove cover and pour 2 Tbsp goma-miso sauce over chicken. Cook for another minute. Remove chicken from pan and set aside to cool.

5. Cover your hand with cling wrap and take one-quarter of the rice into your hands. Make a 2-cm (1-in) indentation in the rice with your finger and add a pinch of shredded cabbage and 2–3 pieces of chicken.

6. Gently press rice 2–3 times into a ball. Make sure the rice completely covers the filling. Remove cling wrap and leave rice balls on a plate to cool. Repeat with the remaining ingredients.

7. Spread a layer of the remaining goma-miso sauce on top of the rice balls. Grill in a toaster oven or frying pan until brown on both sides. Sprinkle white sesame seeds to garnish.

Makes

Chicken breast fillets 1, about 200 g (7 oz) each

Salt 1/4 tsp

Freshly ground black pepper a pinch

Vegetable oil 1 Tbsp

Sake 1 Tbsp

Cooked Japanese short grain rice (see page 18) 400 g (14 1/3 oz)

Cabbage 1/8 head, shredded

Toasted white sesame seeds to garnish

Goma-miso sauce

Miso paste 3 Tbsp

Mirin 3 Tbsp

Toasted white sesame seeds 2 Tbsp, ground

Chopped Japanese leek (*naga negi*) 2 Tbsp

Shiitake Yaki Onigiri

It sounds weird but I feel very proud of shiitake mushrooms every time I see them used in Western cooking programmes and recipe books. It is one of the few Japanese ingredients that has become widely used outside of Japan. It has a unique taste and aroma and I love to use it in soups. It goes well with a variety of seasonings and ingredients. What's more, it is very nutritious!

Makes

Fresh shiitake mushrooms 8

Cooked Japanese short grain rice (see page 18) 480 g (17 oz)

White radish (*daikon*) leaves 20-cm (8-in), blanched, drained and cut into 0.5-cm (1/4-in) lengths

Japanese soy sauce (shoyu) 2 Tbsp + more for brushing on mushrooms

Toasted white sesame seeds 2 Tbsp + more for coating

Salt 1/2 tsp

1. Wipe shiitake mushrooms clean with a damp cloth and remove stems. Score the tops of the mushrooms with an X. Set aside.

2. Combine rice, white radish leaves, soy sauce, sesame seeds and salt in a bowl and mix well.

3. Place cling wrap in a rice bowl and scoop one-eighth of the rice mixture into the bowl. Pull out rice together with cling wrap and mould rice into a ball. Flatten top and bottom of the rice ball slightly. Remove cling wrap. Repeat to make another 7 rice balls.

4. Coat the sides of the rice balls with toasted sesame seeds.

5. Top each rice ball with a shiitake mushroom.

6. Grill rice balls with the mushroom side down in an oven toaster or frying pan for 3 minutes. Turn rice balls over and grill the other side for another 3 minutes or until browned.

7. Brush soy sauce over shiitake mushrooms and grill again until brown on both sides. Brush soy sauce over shiitake mushrooms once again and serve immediately.

Corn Cheese Yaki Onigiri

Whenever I'm at the beach in Japan, I can't resist buying a cob of corn to enjoy. It is one of the most popular types of food you can find at the beach in summer. They are charcoal-grilled and brushed with soy sauce. It's a very simple way of cooking but it tastes fantastic! The corn is very sweet and goes really well with the aroma of soy sauce. The first time I made this onigiri was for my 6-year-old nephew. He didn't like vegetables at all, so I mixed corn with his favourite cheese to make an onigiri. It was a success — he loved it!

1. Remove corn kernels from corn cob. Bring a pot of water to the boil and add a pinch of salt. Cook corn kernels for 4–5 minutes.

2. Put corn, rice, Mozzarella, soy sauce and pepper in a bowl and mix well.

3. Place cling wrap in a rice bowl and scoop one-quarter of the rice mixture into the bowl. Pull out cling wrap together with rice and mould rice into your preferred shape. Remove cling wrap. Repeat with the remaining ingredients.

4. Melt butter in a frying pan and grill rice balls on both sides until brown. Serve hot.

Note This is my grandma's tip for removing corn kernels from the corn cob easily. Remove a line of corn kernels lengthwise using a knife. Using your thumb, push the second line of corn kernels towards first line. The kernels will come off instantly.

Makes

Sweetcorn ¹/₂ ear

Salt a pinch

Cooked Japanese short grain rice (see page 18) 400 g (14¹/₃ oz)

Grated Mozzarella 120 g (4¹/₄ oz)

Japanese soy sauce (shoyu) 4 Tbsp

Freshly ground black pepper to taste

Butter 40 g (1¹/₂ oz)

Cheese Okaka Yaki Onigiri

Cheese, bonito flakes and soy sauce make a delicious combination. I like grilling this onigiri to enjoy the crunch of the grilled rice and melting cheese but it can also be served without grilling.

Makes

Cooked Japanese short grain rice (see page 18) 480 g (17 oz)

Bonito flakes 10 g ($^1/_3$ oz)

Grated Mozzarella 120 g (4$^1/_2$ oz)

Japanese soy sauce (shoyu) 2 Tbsp + more for brushing on onigiri

1. Put rice and bonito flakes in a bowl and mix well. Add Mozzarella and soy sauce and continue to mix well.

2. Place cling wrap in a rice bowl and scoop one-quarter of the rice mixture into the bowl. Pull out rice together with cling wrap and gently mould rice into your preferred shape. Remove cling wrap. Repeat with the remaining ingredients. Leave rice balls on a plate to cool.

3. Brush rice balls with soy sauce and grill in an oven toaster or frying pan until brown on both sides. Brush soy sauce on both sides again and grill for another 10 seconds on each side.

Okonomiyaki Onigiri

One of the most famous dishes from in the Kansai region is *okonomiyaki*. I'm originally from Kansai and *okonomiyaki* is a favourite with my family members. We often cook it at home on weekends. Normally, *okonomiyaki* is a made with flour and lots of cabbage, however, here is an onigiri version you can prepare quickly and easily at home. Plenty of *okonomiyaki* sauce and bonito flakes make this onigiri taste (and look) like *okonomiyaki*!

Makes

Cooked Japanese short grain rice (see page 18) 480 g (17 oz), cooled

Green nori powder (*aonori*) 4 tsp

Dried sakura shrimps (*sakura ebi*) 2 tsp

Store-bought *okonomiyaki* sauce or *tonkatsu* sauce to taste

Mayonnaise to taste

Bonito flakes 10 g (1/3 oz)

Pickled ginger (optional) for garnishing

1. Put rice, green nori powder and dried cherry shrimps in a bowl and mix well.

2. Place cling wrap in a rice bowl and scoop one-quarter of the rice mixture into the bowl. Pull out rice together with cling wrap and mould rice into a ball, then flatten the sides to form a patty. Remove cling wrap.

3. Preheat the frying pan and pan-fry rice patties on both sides until browned. Remove from heat and transfer rice patties to a plate.

4. Spread *okonomiyaki* or *tonkatsu* sauce on top of rice patties. Top with a dollop of mayonnaise, a pinch of bonito flakes and 1/2 Tbsp pickled ginger. Serve immediately.

Note This is an open style onigiri. If you like to pack it in a lunchbox, make smaller rice patties and spread *okonomiyaki* sauce, mayonnaise, bonito flakes and pickled ginger in between 2 rice patties and wrap with cling wrap.

Let's Cook Special Rice
for Our Onigiri

Shio Kombu Fried Rice Onigiri

My mum used to make this for me on Saturdays when I was in elementary school (I had to go to school for half the day on Saturdays!). The aroma of fried soy sauce always reminds me of this fried rice. Kelp is rich in umami, which gives a depth of flavour even though few ingredients are used. If you like it spicy, add hot pepper or seven-spice seasoning (*shichimi togarashi*) after frying the rice.

Makes

Vegetable oil 1 Tbsp

Cooked Japanese short grain rice (see page 18) 480 g (17 oz), cooled

Seasoned kelp (*shio kombu*) 40 g (1¹/₂ oz)

Ground white pepper to taste

Japanese soy sauce (shoyu) 3 Tbsp

Pickled ginger (see page 54) 2 tsp, thinly sliced

Trefoil (*mitsuba*) to garnish, blanched

Egg crêpe

Eggs 4

Milk 4 Tbsp

Potato starch 4 tsp

1. Start by preparing egg crêpe. Combine eggs, milk and potato starch mixture in a small bowl and mix well.

2. Heat some oil in a frying pan and pour in egg mixture into the pan to form a thin crêpe about 15-cm (6-in) in diameter. Repeat with the remaining egg mixture to make 3 more crêpes. Cut crêpes into 8 rectangular strips measuring about 15 x 2.5-cm (6 x 1-in).

3. In a clean pan, heat some oil and add rice, kelp and pepper. Mix well.

4. Remove from heat and pour in soy sauce from the edge of the pan and mix well into the fried rice. Transfer to a plate.

5. To form onigiri, place cling wrap in a rice bowl and place some pickled ginger and one-eighth of the rice on top. Pull out rice together with cling wrap and mould rice into a barrel shape. Remove cling wrap and wrap rice ball with crêpe. Tie a piece of blanched trefoil around the rice ball to garnish. Repeat with the remaining ingredients.

Note If you are in a hurry, make scrambled eggs from the egg crêpe mixture, then mix with rice, kelp and seasoning and form the mixture into rice balls.

Makes

Butter ¹/₂ Tbsp

Onion ¹/₂, peeled and finely diced

Japanese green pepper (*piman*) 1, seeded and finely diced

Carrot 30 g (1 oz), peeled and finely diced

Minced beef 100 g (3¹/₂ oz)

Minced pork 100 g (3¹/₂ oz)

Japanese curry powder 1 Tbsp + more to taste

Sugar ¹/₂ Tbsp

Japanese soy sauce (shoyu) 1 Tbsp

Sake ¹/₂ Tbsp

Cooked Japanese short grain rice (see page 18) 480 g (17 oz)

Dry Curry Onigiri

Dry curry is perfect for onigiri as it doesn't contain any liquid. When cooking the curry for this onigiri, the aroma is simply irresistible!

1. Heat butter in a frying pan over medium heat and sauté onion until translucent.

2. Add green pepper and carrot and cook for 1–2 minutes.

3. Increase heat and add minced beef and pork and cook until meat changes colour. Add curry powder and mix well. Add sugar, soy sauce and sake and cook until the moisture has evaporated. Add rice to the pan and mix well to combine. Remove from heat.

4. Place cling wrap in a rice bowl and scoop one-eighth of the rice mixture in the bowl. Pull out rice together with cling wrap and mould rice into your preferred shape. Remove cling wrap. Repeat with the remaining ingredients.

Note When adding rice into the other ingredients in this recipe, mix it quickly otherwise the rice will dry up, making it hard to mould the rice balls.

Sweet Potato Onigiri

At my elementary school, each class had its own sweet-potato farm. It was hard work taking care of the farm but we had great fun harvesting and cooking the sweet potatoes every autumn. This was one of the dishes we prepared after the harvest. When I eat this sweet potato onigiri, the memory of my fun schooldays comes rushing back to me.

1. Put rice, water, drained sweet potato, soy sauce, sake and salt into a rice cooker and cook according to the instructions on the rice cooker.

2. When the rice is cooked, add black sesame seeds and butter. Mix well.

3. Place cling wrap in a rice bowl and scoop one-quarter of the rice into the bowl. Pull out rice together with cling wrap and mould rice into your preferred shape. Remove cling wrap. Repeat with the remaining ingredients.

Makes

Washed Japanese short grain rice 400 ml (13$^{1}/_{2}$ oz)

Water 400 ml (13$^{1}/_{2}$ fl oz)

Sweet potato 160 g (5$^{2}/_{3}$ oz), washed, peeled and cut into 1-cm ($^{1}/_{2}$-in) cubes, then soaked in water for 20 minutes

Japanese soy sauce (shoyu) 1 Tbsp

Sake 1 Tbsp

Salt 1 tsp

Toasted black sesame seeds 1 Tbsp

Butter 10 g ($^{1}/_{3}$ oz)

Prawn Nam Pla Takikomi Gohan Onigiri

Takikomi gohan means cooked rice with vegetables, meat or seafood. In Japan, seasonal items go into *takikomi gohan* and it's one of the best ways to enjoy seasonal food. This recipe is a little different from the original version. I've added fish sauce (*nam pla* in Thai) in this recipe, which is mostly used in South East Asian cooking, for extra flavour. I hope this will bring an Asian breeze to your taste buds!

Makes

Washed Japanese short grain rice 400 ml (13$^{1}/_{2}$ oz)

Water 400 ml (13$^{1}/_{2}$ fl oz)

Small prawns (shrimps) or frozen seafood mix 85 g (3 oz), shelled and deveined

Jasmine tea bags 2

Fish sauce 2 Tbsp

Chopped coriander leaves (cilantro) 1 Tbsp

Chopped chives 1 Tbsp

1. Put rice, water, prawns or frozen seafood mix, tea bags and fish sauce into a rice cooker and cook according to the instructions on the rice cooker.

2. When the rice is cooked, take out the tea bags and mix the rice well.

3. Transfer the rice into a bowl and add coriander leaves and chives. Mix well.

4. Place cling wrap in a rice bowl and scoop one-eighth of the rice into the bowl. Pull out rice together with cling wrap and mould rice into a ball. Remove cling wrap. Repeat with the remaining ingredients.

Kayaku Takikomi Gohan Onigiri

Kayaku takikomi gohan is a popular rice dish from the Kansai region in Japan. Originally, the word *kayaku* was the general term for supporting ingredients used in Traditional Chinese Medicine. This word has been adopted to refer to taste-enhancing ingredients used in rice and noodles. Try adding seasonal vegetables to make different varieties of *kayaku takikomi gohan*.

Makes

Japanese soy sauce (shoyu) 3 Tbsp

Mirin 1 Tbsp

Salt ¹/₃ tsp

Chicken thigh fillet 1, about 100 g (3¹/₂ oz), finely chopped

Deep-fried bean curd (*aburaage*) 1, about 60 g (2 oz)

Devil's tongue jelly (*konnyaku*) 100 g (3¹/₂ oz)

Dried shiitake mushroom 3, cleaned and soaked in 300 ml (10 fl oz / 1¹/₄ cups) water for 30 minutes

Washed Japanese short grain rice 400 ml (13¹/₂ oz)

Water 200 ml (6³/₄ fl oz) + more if needed

Burdock (*gobou*) 80 g (3 oz), washed, finely chopped and soaked in water for 10 minutes and drained

Carrot 80 g (3 oz), peeled and chopped

1. Mix soy sauce, mirin and salt in a small bowl. Add chicken and mix well. Leave to marinate for 15 minutes.

2. Pour hot water over deep-fried bean curd to remove excess oil. Wrap deep-fried bean curd with kitchen paper and squeeze using your hands. Cut into 1-cm (¹/₂-in) squares.

3. Pour hot water over devil's tongue jelly to remove any impurities. Cut into 1-cm (¹/₂-in) squares. Boil a small pot of water and blanch devil's tongue jelly for 2–3 minutes. Drain and set aside.

4. Drain shiitake mushrooms and chop finely. Reserve liquid used for soaking mushrooms.

5. Put rice into a rice cooker. Top with deep-fried bean curd, devil's tongue jelly, burdock, shiitake mushrooms and chicken. Measure reserved water from soaking mushrooms and top up with water to make 400 ml (13¹/₂ fl oz) liquid. Add this to the rice cooker. Cook rice according to the instructions on the rice cooker. When the rice is cooked, mix well.

6. Place cling wrap in a rice bowl and scoop one-quarter of the rice mixture into the bowl. Pull out rice together with cling wrap and mould rice into your preferred shape. Remove cling wrap. Repeat with the remaining ingredients.

Ginger Takikomi Gohan Onigiri

I like to prepare this onigiri when I find fresh young ginger in the market as I really enjoy the taste of ginger simply cooked with deep-fried bean curd. If you like, you can add *unagi* (barbecued eel) in the onigiri—they go really well together. This is the perfect onigiri to eat when you need some extra energy or when you feel a cold coming, as eating ginger is known to strengthen the immune system.

1. **Pour boiling water over deep-fried bean curd to remove excess oil. Wrap deep-fried bean curd with kitchen paper and squeeze using your hands. Cut bean curd into thin strips.**

2. **Remove kelp from water and set aside. Reserve water.**

3. **Put rice, deep-fried bean curd, ginger, soy sauce, mirin, sake and salt into a rice cooker. Measure reserved water for soaking kelp and top up with more water to get 400 ml (13¹/₂ fl oz) liquid. Cook according to manufacturer's instructions.**

4. **Place cling wrap in a rice bowl and scoop one-quarter of the rice into the bowl. Pull out rice together with cling wrap and mould rice into your preferred shape. Remove cling wrap. Repeat with the remaining ingredients.**

Note Do not throw away the kelp after using it to make dashi water. It can be recycled to make various kinds of *gohan no tomo* (a dish that goes well with rice). To make seasoned kelp (*shio kombu*) for dishes such as Shio Kombu Fried Rice Onigiri (see page 112), slice 100 g (3¹/₂ oz) kelp thinly and put in a small pot together with 700 ml (23²/₃ fl oz) water, 3 Tbsp Japanese soy sauce (shoyu), 1 Tbsp mirin, 2 Tbsp sugar and 2 tsp rice vinegar. Cook over low heat until water is reduced by three-quarters. Stir with a wooden spoon and continue to cook until liquid has completely evaporated. Leave to cool, then stir in 3 Tbsp bonito flakes. This can be stored in an airtight container in the refrigerator for up to 2 weeks.

Makes

Deep-fried bean curd (*aburaage*) 1, about 60 g (2 oz)

Kelp (*dashi kombu*) 1, about 10 x 10-cm (4 x 4-in), wiped clean and soaked in 200 ml (6³/₄ fl oz) water for at least 2 hours

Washed Japanese short grain rice 400 ml (13¹/₂ oz)

Ginger 60 g (2 oz), peeled and thinly sliced

Japanese soy sauce (shoyu) 3 Tbsp

Mirin 1 Tbsp

Sake 1 Tbsp

Salt a pinch

Water 200 ml (6³/₄ fl oz) + more if needed

Chestnut Takikomi Gohan Onigiri

One of the great excitements of autumn is eating chestnuts!
Fresh chestnuts take time to prepare but they taste so good.
To me, chestnuts are a symbol of cool autumn air and blue skies.
Frozen chestnuts are available at most supermarkets throughout
the year and they are also easy to prepare. I'm introducing a
very simple recipe for chestnut rice but if you'd like to add more
ingredients, chicken, burdock, carrot and deep-fried bean curd
(*aburaage*) are great options.

Makes

Chestnuts 15–25, depending
    on size
Washed Japanese short grain
    rice 400 ml (13¹/₂ oz)
Water 400 ml (13¹/₂ fl oz)
Japanese light soy sauce
    (*usukuchi* shoyu) 2 Tbsp
Mirin 2 Tbsp

1. Cut a small slit on chestnuts. Bring a pot of water to the
boil and remove from heat. Add chestnuts and leave until
water is cool, about 1 hour. Shell chestnuts and cut into
halves. Soak in water for another 20 minutes.

2. Put rice, water, soy sauce, mirin and chestnuts in a
rice cooker and cook rice according to instructions on the
rice cooker.

3. When the rice is cooked, mix it lightly.

4. Place cling wrap in a rice bowl and scoop one-quarter of
the rice into the bowl. Pull out rice together with cling wrap
and mould rice into a ball. Remove cling wrap. Repeat with
the remaining ingredients.

Note I use Japanese light soy sauce (*usukuchi* shoyu) in this
recipe to enjoy the colour and sweetness of the chestnuts.
Light soy sauce has more salt than regular soy sauce, which
brings out the sweetness from the chestnuts.

Chicken Rice Onigiri

Chicken rice is one of my favourite local foods in Singapore. In Japan, chicken rice is known simply as fried rice with chicken and vegetables seasoned with tomato ketchup. This recipe features the Singapore version of chicken rice in the form of an onigiri.

Makes

Water 500 ml (16 fl oz / 2 cups)

Chicken stock granules 2 tsp

Japanese leek (*naga negi*) about 20-cm (8-in)

Chicken breast fillet 1, about 200 g (7 oz)

Washed Japanese short grain rice 400 ml (13^1/$_2$ oz)

Jasmine tea 1 bag

Minced garlic 1 tsp

Minced ginger 2 tsp

Salt ^{1}/$_2$ tsp

Coriander leaves (cilantro) to garnish

1. In a pot, boil water and add chicken stock granules and Japanese leek. Add chicken and cook until chicken changes colour.

2. Remove from heat and set aside to cool. Reserve 400 ml (13^1/$_2$ fl oz) of stock.

3. Combine rice, chicken, reserved water, tea bag, garlic, ginger and salt in a rice cooker and cook according to instructions on the rice cooker.

4. When the rice is cooked, remove tea bag and chicken. Cut chicken into bite-size pieces and return chicken to the rice. Gently mix rice well.

5. Cover your hand with cling wrap and take one-quarter of the rice into your hands. Gently press rice 2–3 times into your preferred shape. Remove cling wrap and garnish with coriander leaves. Repeat with the remaining ingredients.

Brown Rice and Red Bean Onigiri

Brown rice is unpolished rice and is an excellent source of iron, magnesium, vitamins, protein and fibre. Since the bran is still attached to the grains, it needs to be soaked in water for several hours to soften. I love the earthy flavour of brown rice but some people simply do not enjoy the taste of it. To make it more appealing to those who don't like brown rice, I cook it with red beans. Red beans are also a good source of nutrients. Studies have shown that eating red beans may help lower cholesterol. Cooking brown rice is almost the same as cooking regular rice. If you have a pressure cooker, try cooking brown rice with it. The rice will be stickier and softer. Here, I used a regular rice cooker.

Makes

Japanese short grain brown rice 400 ml (13^1/$_2$ oz), washed

Water 680 ml (23 fl oz)

Japanese red beans (*adzuki*) 50 g (1^2/$_3$ oz)

Sake 1 Tbsp

Kelp (*dashi kombu*) 5 x 5-cm (2 x 2-in), wiped with a wet cloth

Toasted black sesame seeds (optional) 2 Tbsp

Salt (optional) 1^1/$_2$ tsp

1. Start preparations a day ahead. Soak brown rice in some water and mix well. Discard water.

2. Without adding water, stir rice with your hand rhythmically 5 times. Add water and rinse 2 more times.

3. Before putting rice into the rice cooker, check the amount of rice with a measuring cup and add 1.7 times water to the rice into rice cooker. If washed rice is 400 ml (13^1/$_2$ fl oz), water should be 680 ml (23 fl oz).

4. Leave rice to soak overnight.

5. On the day of cooking, add washed red beans, sake and kelp in a rice cooker and cook according to the instructions on the rice cooker. When rice is cooked, remove kelp and gently stir through. Set aside.

6. If using, combine sesame seeds and ^{1}/$_2$ tsp salt in a small bowl and mix well. Set aside.

7. Scoop one-quarter of the rice into a rice bowl. Wet your hands and spread a pinch of salt on your palms and fingers. Transfer rice to your hands and gently press rice 2–3 times into your preferred shape. Sprinkle sesame mixture over the rice ball, if desired. Repeat with the remaining ingredients.

128

Glossary

Burdock (*gobou*)

This root vegetable can grow up to 1-m (40-in) in length. It is low in calories and full of nutrients. In Japan, people eat only the roots but the leaves can also be eaten in salads. Burdock is said to lower blood pressure and cholesterol. The root vegetable is in season in April to May and November to February. When choosing burdock, select those coated with soil as the soil keeps the beautiful aroma of the root intact. The best kinds of burdock for cooking are straight with smooth skins. Discard those with cracks in the skin. To store burdock, wrap with newspaper and store it in cool and dry place.

Devil's tongue jelly (*konnyaku*)

This jelly is from the devil's tongue plant, which is part of the taro family. It is also known as konjac. The plant takes about 3 years to grow, reaching an optimum diameter of 30-cm (12-in). This devil's tongue plant cannot be consumed raw and has to be processed before eating. The colour of devil's tongue jelly is normally gray but you will find white and red ones as well. You can also find devil's tongue jelly in noodle form. These are called *shirataki*. Unless it is stated on the packaging, most devil's tongue jelly need to be blanched in boiling water before using. This ingredient contains zero calories but is full of fibre.

Japanese chilli pepper (*togarashi*)

There are many chilli peppers in the world but the most popular type of chilli pepper in Japan is called *takano tsume* (eagle's talons) which is about 3-cm (1²/₃-in) in length and often sold in dried form. It is very spicy with a hint of sweetness. The powdered version is sold as *ichimi togarashi*.

Japanese green pepper (*piman*)

The name *piman* comes from the French word *piment*, which means pepper. These peppers are smaller than regular capsicums and have a thin skin with a bittersweet flavour. This green pepper is full of vitamins. Select peppers with a vibrant hue and shiny, perky skin. These green peppers are very sensitive to water. Store them in a plastic bag in the refrigerator.

Japanese leek (*naga negi*)

The Japanese leek is a little different from regular leek. It is thinner and does not have a hard layer inside. Instead, there is a soft centre that melts when cooked. Taste wise, the Japanese leek is very sweet. There are many varieties of Japanese leeks available in Japan and most of them become sweet when cooked. To store, wrap leek in newspaper or put in a plastic bag and keep in the refrigerator standing up. This will keep the leek fresh for a longer time. You can also chop the leek up and store in the freezer.

Japanese red beans (*adzuki*)

Japanese red beans are rich in protein, fibre and minerals. It is good for controlling high blood pressure and cholesterol and preventing water retention. The best way to get the full benefits of these red beans is to cook it in savoury dishes.

Japanese rice seasoning powder (*furikake*)

Furikake is a general name for seasoning powder to sprinkle on rice. It is usually made with dried fish, egg, vegetable and seaweed. There are so many varieties of *furikake* available at the supermarket. You can also use *furikake* on pasta and toast!

Kelp (*kombu*)

Kelp is low in calories and high in minerals. It is said that it contains 20 times more minerals, seven times more calcium and 35 times more iron than regular milk. When cooking, simply wipe the surface very gently with a wet cloth as the white power on the kelp is the source of its delicious taste. To keep kelp, cut into small pieces and store in an airtight container. There are a few types of kelp:

Ma kombu—One of the highest quality kelp, this thick and wide version is great for making soup stock as it is sweet with a clear appearance.

Rishiri kombu—This is great for making dashi, which is slightly salty with a clear appearance.

Hidaka kombu—This variety is dark green in colour and easy to cook. It is great for making dashi and cooking in dishes.

Myoga ginger flower bud

Myoga ginger flower buds originally came from East Asia and are now cultivated throughout Japan. It is easy to grow at home as well. There are two types of myoga, one is flower bud myoga (*hana myoga*) and the other is young stem myoga (*myogadake*). The best season to obtain myoga ginger flower bud is between July and October. The myoga flower bud boasts an attractive pink and white appearance with a distinctive aroma and a bitter flavour. It can be eaten raw, pickled or cooked. To store myoga flower buds, wrap with kitchen towels, then place in a plastic bag in the refrigerator.

Salted cod roe (*tarako*)

Salted cod roe can be eaten raw or cooked. It is rich in protein and vitamins A and B3. Raw cod roe has a slightly salty and delicate caviar-like taste. Once cooked, it takes on a smoky and sweet flavour. It is often used for onigiri, pastas, potato salads and dips. Salted cod roe can be kept in the freezer for up to 90 days and in the refrigerator for up to 6 days. To defrost, transfer the frozen cod roe to the refrigerator to thaw for 6 hours.

Seaweed (hijiki, wakame and nori)

Dried seaweed is easily available from major supermarkets. You can also get fresh ones if they are in season. Generally, seaweed is high in fibre and minerals. Hijiki seaweed (left) is dark green to black and if often sold in dried form. Before cooking, soak hijiki seaweed in water for 30 minutes and rinse thoroughly. It is often cooked with vegetables and soy beans.

Wakame seaweed (centre) is a green algae easily obtained in dried form. Some of types of wakame don't require soaking in water before cooking, so you can sprinkle them into soups directly. Salted raw wakame is also available when in season and can be eaten as sashimi or in salads.

Nori (right) is a dark green seaweed available in a variety of forms and taste. Nori sheets are produced using a similar process to making paper. There are still companies making nori sheets the traditional way where they dry the sheets in the sun. Nori sheets are often used for sushi, soups and as garnish for rice and noodle dishes.

Shiso leaves (ohba)

There are two types of shiso available in Japan: green (*ohba, aoba, aojiso*) and red (*akajiso*). Shiso is part of the mint family and has a basil-like aroma and taste. It is rich in vitamins and minerals. It is commonly used as a garnish for sashimi as it is thought to help preserve and sterilise foods. Red shiso is used to give umeboshi a red colour. The flower buds from the shiso plant can be used as garnish as well. Shiso leaves are in season in summer but you will be able to find them at supermarkets all year round. The best way to store shiso leaves is to wrap them individually with wet kitchen towels and store in an airtight container in the refrigerator.

Soy bean paste (*miso*)

Miso is made from fermented soy beans, barley or rice mixed with salt and *kohji* (a type of fungus used for making sake). There are many varieties of miso from different regions in Japan. You can also purchase miso kits to make miso at home. Miso is rich in protein and calcium. The best way to keep miso is in the freezer as it won't freeze, or simply store it in the refrigerator.

Soy bean powder (*kinako*)

This is made from roasted, peeled and ground soy beans. It has a natural roasted flavour. The colour varies depending the kind of soy beans used. Yellow *kinako* is made from common soy beans, green *kinako* is made from green soy beans and black *kinako* is made from black soy beans. Soy bean powder is rich in fibre and minerals. It is common practice in Japan to mix soy bean powder into milk for a healthy drink! It is often used in Japanese sweets but *kinako* ice cream and butter are readily available nowadays.

Wasabi

Wasabi, also known as Japanese horseradish, originates from Japan. It grows along shallow rivers near the mountains. Since it requires very clean water to thrive, it is considered one of the most difficult plants to cultivate. Most wasabi sold in powdered or paste forms are made from green-tinted horseradish. Grated wasabi root is used as garnish and seasoning. The leaves and stems of the wasabi are also eaten as pickles and fried in batter. Wasabi root has a distinctive spiciness on the nose but it is sweet in the mouth. Since the heat and fragrance disappears when wasabi is mixed with soy sauce, I don't recommend adding soy sauce to wasabi when eating sushi and sashimi. To enjoy the taste of wasabi, smear some onto sushi or sashimi and then dip it into soy sauce. The best kinds of wasabi root is bright green and feels heavy in the hand. To store fresh wasabi root, wash thoroughly under cold running water, wrap with a damp kitchen towel and cover with cling wrap. Keep in the refrigerator for up to 2 weeks.

White radish (daikon) leaf

White radish leaves can be eaten as well but most supermarkets cut them off to prolong the shelf life of the radish. The leaves are nutritious and can be eaten like any other leafy vegetable when cooked. It can also be sun-dried and ground to make *furikake* powder.

White radish (daikon) sprouts (*kaiware daikon*)

White radish sprouts have a spicy flavour which goes well with meat dishes. They are full of vitamins and minerals. These sprouts are often sold in plastic containers with roots attached. Before using, wash thoroughly under running water and remove the roots. To keep, leave the roots intact and store in the refrigerator.

Afterword

It was a great surprise when Lydia from Marshall Cavendish International (Asia) asked me to write a cookbook about onigiri. We chat a lot about food and baking but I had never thought that I would be a cookbook author. I thought it was a great opportunity to introduce others to onigiri and simple Japanese recipes that can be prepared at home. In addition, I felt it was something I had to do as my family name 稲田 (Inada) means "rice farm" and my first name 早苗 (Sanae) means "young rice sprouts".

When I was young, I didn't like eating plain white rice—I needed to have something on top of it or mixed with other ingredients. When I entered elementary school, lunchtime was one of my least favourite times. The school prepared lunch for us every day and we had rice three times a week. My teacher didn't allow us to leave the table if we didn't finish our meals. I was usually the last one at the table on the days when white rice was served. When I confessed to my mother that I didn't enjoy lunch at school, she advised me to make onigiri. I brought cling wrap to school and made onigiri using side dishes as fillings. Since then, my lunch at school turned out fun and creative. In fact, my schoolmates started making onigiri with me and experimenting with fillings!

My grandma always said, "Don't leave any rice in your rice bowl. If you leave even one grain of rice, you will lose your eye in the future". She often made onigiri with leftover rice. If there were a few rice grains left in my bowl, she would pour hot green tea into it to make sure all the rice grains were washed away when I drank tea. I used to believe my grandma when I was small but after learning how to grow rice and acknowledging the time and effort it takes to prepare meals every day, I understand why my grandma chided me. It's funny that I'm still careful not to leave a single grain of rice in my bowl and I still hear my grandma's voice in my head whenever I'm eating a bowl of rice.

I hope this book inspires you to try making Japanese rice balls. There is no rule in size and ingredients. All you need is delicious rice, salt and creativity!

Weights and Measures

Quantities for this book are given in Metric, Imperial and American (spoon) measures. Standard spoon and cup measurements used are: 1 tsp = 5 ml, 1 Tbsp = 15 ml, 1 cup = 250 ml. All measures are level unless otherwise stated.

Liquid And Volume Measures

Metric	Imperial	American
5 ml	$1/6$ fl oz	1 teaspoon
10 ml	$1/3$ fl oz	1 dessertspoon
15 ml	$1/2$ fl oz	1 tablespoon
60 ml	2 fl oz	$1/4$ cup (4 tablespoons)
85 ml	$2^1/2$ fl oz	$1/3$ cup
90 ml	3 fl oz	$3/8$ cup (6 tablespoons)
125 ml	4 fl oz	$1/2$ cup
180 ml	6 fl oz	$3/4$ cup
250 ml	8 fl oz	1 cup
300 ml	10 fl oz ($1/2$ pint)	$1^1/4$ cups
375 ml	12 fl oz	$1^1/2$ cups
435 ml	14 fl oz	$1^3/4$ cups
500 ml	16 fl oz	2 cups
625 ml	20 fl oz (1 pint)	$2^1/2$ cups
750 ml	24 fl oz ($1^1/5$ pints)	3 cups
1 litre	32 fl oz ($1^3/5$ pints)	4 cups
1.25 litres	40 fl oz (2 pints)	5 cups
1.5 litres	48 fl oz ($2^2/5$ pints)	6 cups
2.5 litres	80 fl oz (4 pints)	10 cups

Dry Measures

Metric	Imperial
30 grams	1 ounce
45 grams	$1^1/2$ ounces
55 grams	2 ounces
70 grams	$2^1/2$ ounces
85 grams	3 ounces
100 grams	$3^1/2$ ounces
110 grams	4 ounces
125 grams	$4^1/2$ ounces
140 grams	5 ounces
280 grams	10 ounces
450 grams	16 ounces (1 pound)
500 grams	1 pound, $1^1/2$ ounces
700 grams	$1^1/2$ pounds
800 grams	$1^1/2$ pounds
1 kilogram	2 pounds, 3 ounces
1.5 kilograms	3 pounds, $4^1/2$ ounces
2 kilograms	4 pounds, 6 ounces

Oven Temperature

	°C	°F	Gas Regulo
Very slow	120	250	1
Slow	150	300	2
Moderately slow	160	325	3
Moderate	180	350	4
Moderately hot	190/200	370/400	5/6
Hot	210/220	410/440	6/7
Very hot	230	450	8
Super hot	250/290	475/550	9/10

Length

Metric	Imperial
0.5 cm	$1/4$ inch
1 cm	$1/2$ inch
1.5 cm	$3/4$ inch
2.5 cm	1 inch